Quench Your Thirst with Salt

D1572435

Quench Your
Thirst with Salt

Essays by

NICOLE WALKER

~~~

ZONE 3 PRESS
Clarksville, Tennessee

The author wishes to thank the following publications in which some of
the essays, in slightly different form, have already appeared: *Crazyhorse,
Ninth Letter, Fourth Genre, Gulf Coast, Shenandoah, Brevity, Seneca
Review,* and *Zone 3.*

Cataloging-in-Publication Data is available from the
Library of Congress. ISBN: 978–0–9786127–7–1

Book design by Dariel Mayer
Cover design and Illustration by David Bieloh

Excerpt from "Water: Too much may be as bad as too little" by Anastasia Stephens.
© 2001 by *The Independent*. Reprinted by permission of *The Independent*. Excerpt
from "Endothelin-1 synthesis reduced by red wine." © 2001 by *Nature News*.
Reprinted by permission of Macmillan Publishers Ltd., and the author. Excerpt from
NPR® news report titled "The Battle Over Water Rights" was originally published
on August 28, 2003, and is used with permission from NPR. © 2003 National Public
Radio, Inc. Excerpt from Linda Sillitoe's *A History of Salt Lake County*, 1996,
published by the Utah State Historical Society and the Salt Lake County Commission.
Reprinted by permission of Utah.gov. Excerpt from "Alcohol and Heart Disease"
can be found on the website of the Women's Heart Foundation. For sources, visit
http://goo.gl/h0jKun. Excerpt from "Oolitic Sand on Stansbury Island, Tooele
County." Used by permission of the Utah Geological Survey, a division of the Utah
Department of Natural Resources. Excerpt from "An Analysis of Utah Oil and Gas
Production, Leasing, and Future Resources." Copyright © 2011 Mark Lemkin.
Reprinted by permission of the Southern Utah Wilderness Alliance. Excerpt from
"Las Vegas Geology Highlights." © 2013 Andrew Alden (*http://geology.about.com/*).
Used with permission from About Inc., which can be found online at *www.about.
com*. All rights reserved. Excerpt from "Water, Water Everywhere." Copyright ©
OPB.org. Reprinted with permission from Oregon Public Broadcasting. Excerpts
from "Hydrologic Activity." Reprinted by permission of the National Park Service/
Glen Canyon NRA. Excerpts from "The Los Angeles Dam Story." Courtesy of the
Department of the Interior. Excerpt from "Instinct Is Not Evil" (June 26, 2005). © 2005
by *The Salt Lake Tribune*. Reprinted by permission of *The Salt Lake Tribune*.

Austin Peay State University, a TBR institution, is an AA/EEO employer
and does not discriminate on the basis of race, color, national origin,
sex, disability or age in its program and activities.

To my dad, who couldn't make it.
And to my mom, who could.

CONTENTS

INTRODUCTION

Alan Weisman suggests in *The World Without Us* (an imaginative/ scientific investigation into a world that's finally shaken us off), that the dream of restoring the land to its "original" state is impossible. To do so, we'd have to renounce and untangle ourselves from every imaginable system that defines us today. In fact, to turn a forest back in time even 200 years, we'd need to eradicate all foreign flora and fauna, swear off future imports, wait for generations of creatures to finish consuming and delivering hidden seeds, and even then, should we manage to give up all industry immediately, we'd not be able to rid the ground, water, and air of heavy metal contamination. What we know to be true emotionally, Weisman asserts scientifically: you can't go home again.

Nicole Walker has her own take on the matter.

Compelled to live in a new, holistic way, and driven to understand the complicated, haunting landscape of her youth, Walker undertakes the heroic project of return. In *Quench Your Thirst with Salt,* the dream of restoration is replaced by the art of reflection, revealing a tender kinship between humans and a land both exposed to corrosive, disfiguring forces. Walker creates a language for and nurtures an imagination about the land in order to align herself intimately with a compromised place. She is also willing to "reform," as land does, in response to pressures of rapid growth, negligence, misuse. The word "reform" here is key to understanding the scope of Walker's journey. In it, you'll hear definitions and echoes of the kinds of endeavors she undertakes: *to remake a spirit that's lost shape; to renounce destructive past habits in favor of healthier*

ones; to start again at the beginning and make from scratch. Nicole
Walker's reforming of self and land might also be seen as a *reclamation* and a *rededication*—terms we use to indicate partnership, to
arrest dissolution, to claim stewardship, and to indicate our pledge
to renew the energy necessary to care.

Quench Your Thirst with Salt asserts a powerful, primary truth:
the body *is* the land. It's not just that the body and land metaphor-
ically reflect one another (though this stance is indeed the book's
guiding premise) but rather, one is also *physically* marked by the
land of one's childhood. To feel a place "in the bones" means something particular for Walker. Land and place participate in our understanding of the shapes and limits, the contours and precipices and
thresholds of our core selves. If we are lucky we can return to the
memory of a childhood home and find there a sense of sanctuary and
a history that sets us alongside generations, and provides us with
solid foundations. More often than not though, the land's beauty and
health is endangered, and its history complex, up-ending even—and
we are left searching amid ruins for a sense of wholeness. Recently, I
was asked to define my "chosen place"—a place I returned to for sustenance. I wanted to be able to say "the beaches of my childhood,"
and while many of Long Island's beaches *are* well-kept and peaceful,
they're also compromised by commerce encroaching on fragile waterways, pollution from refineries, and suburban sprawl. West Vir-
ginians look out on mountains and hollows that at first glance seem
intact, but when viewed from above resemble war zones, blown
apart and poisoned from devastating mining practices. Nicole Walker's chosen place is similarly complex in its physical and existential
dangers. Held by this land—the brutal, the misused, the strangely
compelling—she seeks to reinhabit it *all,* without illusion, straight
on, and with an open spirit, heart, and intellect.

The essay, as Nicole Walker practices it, is a form especially
well-equipped to suggest that the body and land are one ecosystem.
How does she do this? By resisting techniques that let a writer off
easily (gratuitous cutting and splicing, fragmenting, mashing up—
curses of an age afraid to commit to the rigors of creation and au-
thentic feeling), and by proving that the essay, in the right hands,

can indeed make good and practical use of disparate-seeming parts. You'll find within these pages a variety of elements necessary to her project: charts and photos; prose poem-like sections; lists; hard research; sharp juxtapositions; memoir-scenes, painful and tender confessional moments—all bound by a commitment to shapely language. Nicole Walker manages the daunting task of moving briskly from personal story to hard fact by asserting that *both* are necessary to engage her subjects fully and accurately. This dual task could only be successfully accomplished by a writer who believes that the body of land we live on, and the land that's migrated into our bodies, are one and the same entity, in need of protection, understanding, and yes, hard won adoration.

Lia Purpura
Loyola University

Fish

1

The fish jumped a ladder built of electricity and concrete. Swimming up the Columbia teaches her a lesson about progress. Even before the dam, the waterfalls would have battered her forefathers. The rocks would have walloped a punch, broken the skin, bruised the flesh. Now the flesh starts bruised, already whaled on by 40 pounds per inch spray kept narrow and forceful by the steel holes boring through 200 feet of cement. The water directs her toward the spillway. She directs her body against the current.

All the roe she had to hoe.

Eggs lined up in her tubes. Red roe. Follicular. Funicular. She looked at the cables of fire streaming above her. Follicles polishing those little apples.

Apple of her eye. Her silver skin turning apple-skin—ripening. Dying. Water polishing the concrete to a smooth, slippery, no holds, no nook, no rub step.

She flipped her body up the next.

Ten more flights to go.

Share a step with another salmon.

She had swum by him a while ago.

Now he swims in circles.

She has to jump over him as well as the stair.

Head over fin.

2

I am eleven years old and holding onto a fishing pole, trolling for big fish in the deep water off Florida's coast. I must have been beautiful then. Three grown men stood around me. One with a stubbly beard lifted my feet and placed them in the hold. To hold on. To get leverage. To bear down.

The other man, with a pair of sunglasses on his face and another on a pair of chums around his neck, held my hand, folded it around the handle of the reel.

My father stood to my left, cheering me on.

Don't let it go. It's huge. Hold on tight.

Sunglass man pulled my hand toward my body, then out to sea. Following the turbines of the engine. Circling.

The fish, as it jumped out of the water, arched its back. It looked stubbly faced man in the eyes.

Sunglass-man held the fish. Stubbly man hit the fish over the head.

No one eats forty-eight inch barracuda.

They throw it in the cooler anyway.

3

Cooking filets of fish is not complicated. Salt and pepper the fish. Press the water out of the skin with a knife. Slide it across at a twenty-degree angle. In the pan, in some oil, two minutes on the skin side, one minute on the flesh.

It's the sauce that's difficult.

First you need an herb rarely paired with food like rue or lavender or chamomile.

Sometimes green tea. Or demi-glace.

Then you need an emulsion. One stick of butter per dinner party. OK, maybe two.

Reduce the green tea or lobster body fish stock. Or warm the demi-glace.

Strain through a chinois. Strain through cheese cloth. Strain one more time for good measure.

With a steel whip, turn in a cube of butter. Don't let it melt. Emulsify means to unite as one. Make the reduction open up and hook elbows with a molecule of the fat. Water and oil don't mix, my ass. Water and oil are the same thing, if you whisk fast enough and if you add the butter slowly.

Puddle the emulsion in the middle of the plate.

Pile under the fish some truffled risotto, some roasted potatoes, some chard wilted in wine.

For color add citrus or tomatoes or little dices of carrot, strewn around the plate.

Let the fish rest for a minute or so. To re-distribute the juices. To firm the flesh. Do not let the fish get cold.

Superfluidity

A glass of water

The sound of ice-machine shaking out cubes interrupts the TV.

No one tells Dad to be quiet as he might tell us.

The blinds are closed so the windows don't reflect in the screen, keeping the room dark except for the blue light of the tube focusing its stream of electrons. On-location scenes light up each of our faces. Mom nested in the corner of the couch. Paige and Val on their stomachs on the floor, hands under chin, feet in the air. I sit in a rocking chair, next to Dad's over-stuffed. J.R. Ewing sits on the white fence of the horse corral. His teeth grit when he tells Bobby that no amount of Pam's whining will convince him to sell.

Dad is filling his water glass for what must be the thirteenth time that night. Dad drinks a lot of water. He has water for breakfast, before he leaves for work, and starts drinking it again the minute he comes home. He's always telling Mom to drink more water. You'll live longer, he tells her. Then he goes to check on the sprinkler box in the garage. Glass of ice-water in hand. It is full to the brim.

WHAT ARE YOU MADE OF?
By Anastasia Stephens
The Independent—London
11/6/2001

Want to flush out toxins, get rid of cystitis, lose weight and look younger? Look no further than your tap.

According to women's magazines, most supermodels and
my girlfriends, the answer couldn't be simpler. Water. Drink
at least 2 liters a day, more if you can. As for detox, it's a
virtual panacea; most health spas these days offer waterings
at both ends.

My mom told me, after they divorced, that Dad kept a half-gallon
of Absolut in the trunk of his car. Half of those glasses of ice-water
could have been vodka. Maybe more than half.

Hawaii

Green folded inside of white folded inside of blue. An elegant nap-
kin. A vacation is a crease, a bump or a crevasse, depending on how
it unfolds.

We are allowed to swim everywhere. We are eight and eleven
and each of us swims for the swim team back home. We dive in the
shallow water, looking for seashells that haven't been tossed on the
shore yet. Dad and Mom are on the beach, reading. There are no seashells, just a smooth blanket of sand that seems far away when we
look at it underwater. Our eyes sting with the salt but we keep them
open all the same. The waves are big but we know how to body surf.
Since we can stand in this shallow water, we bend our knees, turn
our heads and jump toward the shore to ride on top of the wave.

We jump over the waves, swimming back out to their crests. We
go a little farther this time. We jump and land and then Val screams.
In between the foam of the waves, blood rises up. We panic and think
shark, and the waves push us back in.

She has stepped on some coral. Her foot is sliced and spilling
clean blood. Hobbling, she cries for Mom. Dad jumps up but Mom
says, it'll be fine, it just needs a Band-Aid. She tells him to stay here
with Paige and me. Dad tells us to watch out for coral. So we do.
We swim instead of jump. I'm still looking for sharks—the blood is
still in the water. We swim out further to avoid the near-shore coral.
Pretty soon, we can't touch the ocean floor. Pretty soon, I look down

and I can't even see the ocean floor. We are in a rip tide. We have fallen off the sandbar. No matter how hard I swim, the further out we seem to go.

"Don't panic," I tell Paige. "You get on my back. Wave and yell at Dad. I'll swim us back like dolphins."

So Paige is yelling, "Dad help!" and I'm swimming breast-stroke, all the while keeping my eyes peeled for sharks. We can barely see Dad, but he seems to be waving at us.

OR ARE YOU MADE OF THIS?
Red wine may suppress one of the main chemical culprits
in heart disease.
20 December 2001
ERICA KLARREICH

Indulging in a little fine Cabernet Sauvignon this Christmas could well do you good. Red wine blocks a cellular compound thought to be a key factor in heart disease, a new study finds, bolstering claims that red wine carries more health benefits than other alcoholic beverages.

The finding may help explain why the French, who often drink red wine with meals, appear to have a lower risk of heart disease than people in Britain despite eating a similar amount of saturated fat—a phenomenon known as the 'French paradox.'

Dad did see us when he put his glasses on. He swam out to us in big, broad strokes. Pulling Paige onto his back, he looked at me to ask if I could go on by myself. I nodded as much as I could without getting water in my nose and started swimming.

Evanston, Wyoming

I woke up as the sun was rising right out of my head. I tried to swat it off but my fingers hit lace curtains instead. Landing on something warm but not nearly sun-hot, my fingers touched something solid. Wood, not aluminum, windowsill. The blue of this room was not the blue of my room at home. This blue came through the lace like a shock. The pushy blue-sky of Wyoming. A suitcase that Mom had packed hurriedly for me sat by the door. We weren't here for just the day.

I could hear Mom and Great-grandma through the steel vents that pushed the heat from the downstairs up toward the second floor. An old Victorian house in Evanston, Wyoming. This was my mother's house. She inherited it from her dad's parents after he died in a shoot-out in Ogden. The cops told him to leave the bar. He wanted one last drink. Some banker became my mother's trustee, schemed her and my aunts out of a few thousand dollars, but set this house up for them to live in. Which they did. Along with my grandma, Grandma's three sisters and four brothers, and my great-grandma. My mother and her sisters left it behind when my grandma moved to Salt Lake. Now, it was my great-grandmother's house and it smelled of overheated rooms and newly folded afghans.

I wasn't sure if I was allowed to leave the room but I didn't want to listen to Mom explain why we were there to Great-grandma. My head felt the pang of it; I didn't need the ringing shame to boot. Trying not to make the stairs creak, for the sake of my head as much as any incipient confrontation, I headed out the front door to look for my sisters. Instead of finding them, I found my grandma who had also come up from Salt Lake to see if anything could be done. She knew what I had done. I could see it in her face. Taking two steps back, I turned from her and ran upstairs toward the bathroom to throw up. A one-bathroom house for all those people. This time, the bathroom was unoccupied. I didn't know how lucky I was at the time. But those vents. They were like megaphones. The first parts of the sentences were muffled but the last rang like church bells.

"how drunk?"

"worse than I'd ever seen."

"while Nikki was baby-sitting."

"You know where she got it."

"drink anything."

"anything for attention."

"lucky nobody got killed."

"not going back."

Not going back? Was Dad on his way up here with all our couches and books? I went back onto the bed in the room that I supposed would be mine now and tried not to watch the white ceiling spin pink. I remembered drinking the crème de menthe and Jack Daniels Linda had made for me. I remembered the kids waking up and asking me if I was sick. I don't remember Dean and Gail coming home to see me throwing up all over their white carpet or seeing anyone yell at Linda, who, I suppose, wasn't nearly as bad off as I. I remember getting in the back of my mom's Jeep and lying on one of my sisters' laps as streetlights flashed through the backseat windows. And then I was in this room with the white curtains and the white bedspread and white pillow shams wondering how anyone could leave me alone with anything white again. I returned to the pink bathroom. I covered the vent with all the towels I could find and laid on top of them. I could still hear their voices but they could be talking about anything—sweet peas or Uncle Dick or the squirrel bowl I'd stolen three years ago when I was little. I thought about living here, in Evanston, Wyoming, where it was drier than Salt Lake City and the wind blew two-hundred days of the year.

YOU COME FROM A PLACE OF SCARCITY

VanCampen is a water cop; his job is to make sure those who have the most senior right to what little water flows down the Musselshell River get it, no matter where they are on the river. Last year, VanCampen caught one rancher illegally trying to irrigate his parched fields. The rancher's water right dated back to 1900, but only those with rights dating to 1883 or before had priority access to water at the time.

—From NPR®, "The Battle Over Water Rights," August 28, 2003

I didn't know until just last year that we didn't go to Evanston because of me. We went because that was the night my dad had gotten his first DUI. Mom told him if he didn't quit drinking, she was leaving him. Was that the night he said he'd stop? I can't remember.

Snow

Every Sunday, in the winter, we went skiing. Mom would sometimes go, but usually it was just Dad and me and the twins. Sometimes just Dad and me. We went to Alta which was small and, Dad thought, had better snow and fewer crowds. And, I thought, colder.

On a particularly cold Sunday in the beginning of January, the twins and Dad and I headed up the canyon. The sky was black with heavy snow. As we packed the car with poles and boots, gloves and skis, Mom kept checking the weather. The road could be closed, she warned Dad. You guys sure you want to go? She asked the twins. You don't have to. But we did have to. Dad had asked us the night before. He didn't like to change plans. We were already up. We didn't like to change plans either. We had eaten Cheerios and, dressed in our long underwear, we were shoveling Blistex and hats into our ski bags. We were hot just looking for our ski socks. Of course, it would be plenty warm when we were on the slopes.

Dad drove Mom's Jeep Cherokee past the sign at the mouth of the canyon. Chains or four-wheel drive required. He slid the Jeep into four-high. We turned up Simon and Garfunkel and sang loudly. Dad rarely sang but when he did, his deep bass voice made us laugh. Barry White, if we had known Barry White's voice. But we only knew Paul Simon's alto. Dad could not hit the high notes of "Bridge Over Troubled Water" but he could do a pretty good "Fifty Ways to Leave Your Lover." At least the talky parts.

The wind sucked all the moisture out of our cheeks. We hurried back in the car to put on our hats and try to find facemasks that Dad always told us made us look like bank robbers. They smelled and tasted like last year's snow. Dad just pulled his turtleneck up tighter. Ski-mask or turtle-neck, it didn't matter; the condensation between fabric and mouth would become a bridge of ice crystals. We each had an extra pair of socks, but only Valerie had glove liners. She promised she would share with Paige and me. Dad said we may as well get going to warm up. The wind was pushing us toward the chair lift anyway.

By the third run, Dad rode with me up the lift. I told him my hands were numb. He took off one of my gloves and stuck my hand inside his glove, warming it up. Then he warmed up the other one. In the chair behind us, you could see the twins huddling together. When we got off the lift, Val had tears in her eyes. Dad told her not to cry. The tears would freeze to her face. She laughed a little and Dad said, well, at least we're the only ones here today. All this powder. We hurried to put our hands through the loops of our poles and followed Dad across the bowl.

My legs were too frozen to make the first turn. I kept skiing across. Even the twins, who had been skiing three years fewer than I, had managed to point their tips downhill, hop to the right and make it past the steepest part of the mountain. But I was sure my shins would break at the knees like icicles off rain gutters. I couldn't go any further. The bowl ended in a sheer rock face. I had to do what my dad did sometimes when he had to ski back toward where one of my sisters or I had fallen. I took my downhill ski, pointed the tip up toward the sky, and swung it toward the chairlift. Ballet's third position. Then I took my other ski and brought it parallel to the first. I skied downhill a little, but basically followed my original tracks across the mountain. Dad and the twins waited for me at the bottom of the hill. I could tell they were cold. I tried to hurry, but I had to do one more three-point, hip-twist turn-out. By the next slide across the bowl, I was down low enough to make a normal turn. I finally made it down to them. Dad's goggles had fogged and the twins' lips were blue.

YOU COME FROM A PLACE OF SCARCITY AND ABUNDANCE. PERHAPS THIS IS YOUR PROBLEM.

The 1981–82 water year had broken all records; then September 1982 climaxed with ten times more moisture than normal. A sense of foreboding grew valley-wide, as autumn mud slides closed Big and Little Cottonwood canyons and creeks flooded, damaging three hundred homes, roads, and bridges. At September's end, Governor Matheson declared a state of emergency, but the federal government declined his appeal for aid.

Over the Memorial Day weekend, temperatures rose into the 90s. Children and teenagers splashed in the swollen creeks, ponds, and even the new river. . . .

We didn't want to waste Dad's money. I didn't want him to think I was as cold as Paige and Val. But the snow was falling so hard we couldn't see the ridges in the snow. I had fallen and gotten my hat wet. Dad's teeth were chattering. The lodge was crowded even at ten that morning. Dad bought us cider and French fries as we wasted good money trying to decide whether or not to take another run.

The Rhein

Everyone's bags are packed except mine. My mom tries to braid Paige's hair as she hurries her down the hallway. I'm packing slowly. Dad comes to see what's the hold up. I'm folding the same shirt over and over again. Couldn't you do that last night?

Last night I had to see David. I talked to him. I've decided I'm not going.

Dad can't believe I said what I am saying. I'm not going to Europe.

He walks down the hallway, down the stairs. I follow him. I'm serious.

He holds the garage door open for me.

Get in the car, he says. The plane leaves for New York in two hours. His hand grips the door. Mom slides through it with a suitcase. She knows I won't win this fight. Fine, stay, she says. I'll call your grandmother to come babysit.

Get in the car, Dad repeats.

I'm not going. Why couldn't you buy a ticket for David?

I am an ingrate. I am a spoiled rotten little brat. He has worked so hard for this. Every day from six until ten o'clock, he works—six to six at Terra Tek, six to ten in his home office. One of my jobs is to help him with his home office—matching credit card slips to bank statements, preparing tax returns. This is my vacation too and I'm decidedly not going on vacation with my boss.

But you're going with your father, who has only wanted to give you this for his whole life. His whole family for three weeks in Europe. Who can do that? Not his parents. Not Mom's. He has planned this trip for over a year.

Get in the goddamn car.

I'm not leaving David.

Get in the car.

He never yells. Mom's the one who yells. Dad just avoids.

I'll be here when you get back.

Get in the car right now.

Fuck you.

I have never said those words to my dad. And so he does what he never does. He lunges at me. I run back up the stairs to my bedroom. I jump on my bed. I am running away from my dad and he is chasing me. He catches me and spanks me. And I suddenly am seven instead of seventeen and I'm crying into my blue comforter.

Nicole. This is ridiculous. Please come with us. He gets up and walks across the blue carpet that I picked out when I was ten and spilled cough syrup on a week after we moved in, leaving a giant purple bruise. I'm mad, but I've given in. This is the first real interaction my dad and I have had for years. Perhaps I should swear at him more often.

YOU YOURSELF ARE ABUNDANT

Women's Heart Foundation: Most people don't think of
alcohol as a drug . . . but it is. Alcohol abuse has destroyed
more lives, broken apart more families, caused more diseases
and contributed to more auto fatalities than any other drug.
It is the major contributing factor in the growing epidemic of
domestic violence.

More than half of all adults drink, but not everyone who
drinks is an alcoholic. Alcoholism is a complex psychosocial
disease. Those who drink risk becoming an alcoholic. It
impairs your judgement and affects the way you think, feel
and communicate.

Satisfying the urge to drink becomes the top priority
in the alcoholic's life. This urge can become stronger than
sexual needs, stronger than the need to satisfy hunger,
stronger even than the need for survival.

The urge to get high with alcohol becomes linked to
all other aspects of life. Tension, depression, anger and
excitement can all trigger the desire to take a drink.

No matter how long an alcoholic has been sober, he or she
will always be at risk for alcohol abuse. As time passes with
sobriety, the urge to drink weakens and occurs less often, but it
can return with ferocious and overpowering strength at any time.

He has stopped yelling now. Instead, he calmly argues, You are
seventeen. This may be our last trip as a family. David will be here
when we get back.

He takes my suitcase down the hall, down the stairs, puts it in
the trunk of the car where he usually, apparently, hid his vodka.

While we were gone, David came over to our house to mow the lawn
and hit the head of a sprinkler. The sprinklers went on and flooded
the basement. Dad had to have all the carpet pulled up and replaced.
I resumed my job as primary lawn-mower.

SOME RULES TO TRAIN YOUR ABUNDANT SPIRIT

TAVERNS, or BEER BARS   These establishments may sell
  beer no stronger than 3.2% by weight. They need not
  serve food.

AIRPORT LOUNGES   Can serve beer, wine and mixed drinks
  with or without food. There are only a very few of these.
  They are all located at the Salt Lake International Airport
  and are intended to give visitors a warm first impression.

BREW PUBS   Serve beer which was brewed on premises.
  There are some of these in the state.

RESTAURANTS   With the proper license, alcoholic
  beverages may be served with meals. Liquor bottles must
  be hidden from view. Servers are not allowed to solicit or
  suggest drinks. Patrons must request a wine list or drink
  menu. If a restaurant derives more than 30% of its profit
  from alcoholic beverage sales it can lose its license.

PRIVATE CLUBS   Beer, wine and mixed drinks may be
  consumed in non-exclusive private clubs between 10:00
  a.m. and 1:00 a.m. These clubs by law must be non-profit
  organizations, must charge a membership fee and are
  barred from advertising to boost membership.

The Rules We Can't Obey

The last time I talked to my dad before he died, he called me at 2:30
in the morning, around his birthday.

Good morning.

Dad, it's two in the morning, three for you in Salt Lake.

No, it's not. It's 9 o'clock. How late do people in Portland sleep
in anyway?

Dad, look outside. It's dark. Call me when it's light out.

Nik, I have to tell you something. (Here, his words started
to slur.)

What do you have to tell me that can't wait until morning?

Nik, I've won all the awards I'm going to win.

That's not true, Dad.

I have patents.

I know.

I don't have a job anymore.

I know, Dad. But you can get a new job. Write a book.

I'm in Who's Who.

I know, Dad. But think. You might have grandchildren soon. That's an award in a way.

My diamond drill bit is in the Smithsonian.

You still have us, Dad. Me and the twins. It's almost your birthday.

I know, Nik. But there are no more awards.

PERHAPS YOU COULD EMPLOY
SOME SELF-MODERATION

You can lead a horse to water,
but you can't make him drink.
You can lead a community to save water,
but you can't make us think.
The water-use restrictions passed Tuesday by the Salt Lake
County Council are more about leading than about making.
But this action, and other examples of leadership around the
state, should at least get people to be thinking about the ways
in which we use, and waste, water every day.
If we don't, then much more stringent conservation laws will
come into play. Our leaders will have no choice.
So slow down. The water you save will be your own.

It rained in Portland from the day of my dad's fiftieth birthday—September 22nd—until his funeral on October 26th. I flew home to Salt Lake to blue skies and brown trees. When I saw him lying on the table in the morgue, he looked frozen. Curled in a fetal ball with just one little bruise on his forehead. They didn't do an autopsy. They didn't fill him with formaldehyde. They would have to stretch him out before they cremated him. I left him alone and went looking for something to drink. I was thirsty.

Filtered Water

I wonder where the water goes every time I flush the toilet. I mean, I know where it goes—down the pipes, through the walls, to the stack in the basement. A larger pipe takes the water out to the sewer. The sewer line takes it to the water treatment plant. I'm still amazed that a little gravity—no electricity required—can force not only water but also disposaled food and toilet paper, toothpaste, shit, flush floss, gum and each page of those daily calendars that show 365 Sniglets, Quotable Quotes, Days of Beer, or little known trivia of the North Pole, out of the house, under the street, and down fourteen miles. But where does it end up?

It turns out that not only flushed and drained stuff needs to be treated at your local water treatment facility. Even the water that goes down storm drains needs to be put through the system. Think of all the stuff that runs down the street—golf balls, engine oil, Wendy's wrappers. Even dead animals find their way down the storm drain. And sometimes mice, captured in a mousetrap or by the house cat or even caught alive, find their swirling way down the toilet bowl. So first, according to the USDA, at the local water treatment facility, the water is filtered through a series of screens which act like soil to filter out the solids, sending the somewhat cleaner water downstream. What happens to the solids? I imagine they bury them or send them to the landfill. Perhaps they should stuff MX missiles with the stuff. Think of the savings. We could have repelled the Russians with repulsion. Actually, I research later, it turns out that special bacteria eat the solids and break them down into what I guess you would call, new dirt.

Then, also mimicking nature's natural filtration system, the water-treaters aerate the urine-y water with hundreds of pipes forcing air through—just like a river rushing down steep mountains and over boulders. Sedimentation tanks act like small lakes and ponds. The scum—grease, oils, soaps and plastic—floats to the top and is raked off the surface. In nature, we call these rakes "birds" or maybe "clouds." Then, chlorine is added to kill all the bacteria. Chlorine acts like algae, breaking the nitrogen away from whatever salt has been flushed or used to melt snow. The sun scours. Chemicals are, like everything else, natural.

After this fast-track, the water is put back on its original course. The wastewater, which is now just plain, if doctored, water, is drained into a local river or waterway. Although some water must be lost to the solids and the rakes, most of it makes it back downstream. The added electricity for screening and aerating, the added chemicals, the unknown location of the leftover sludge and scum may provide some cause for concern about human-meddling, but the water is still there. So flush away. You're not wasting. Just recycling.

Apocryphal Story 1

There are so many things I don't know. I don't know how old my mom was when her dad died. I don't know exactly what my dad's dad died of. I don't know what color hair either grandfather had or whether they loved or even liked being with their kids. Were their voices gruff, gravely, tired, accented?

By the time I'm a year old, both my grandfathers are dead. Although there's a portrait of my dad's dad above my grandmother's television of him in his army uniform, I don't believe it really is him. He's surrounded in a white cloud of background and his brown uniform and brown cap and various insignia make him look presidential. I doubt if he was president material. I don't even know if he was a good soldier. Both my grandfathers flew planes in World War II. Both of them survived the war so each of them could produce my parents and then die later. Not all that much later, in my mom's dad's case.

I don't know what my grandpa on my mom's side looked like at all—not even an angelic version of him. When I was little, I pictured that he looked like a pirate or a musketeer. When my mother talked about him to her mother and grandmother, which she rarely did, she spoke as if their house in Evanston was an island and he had touched those shores only in the night, to steal a kiss, or some money, or a pint.

Apocryphal Story 2

I am three and my father is gone, out of town. My mother is pregnant with twins. When my dad returns, he'll bring me a plastic doll from Germany with a green skirt and blond braids to add to my collection. I have a Swedish doll, a French doll, a Native American doll. Although I don't think he ever made it to Native America. Maybe Montana. My mother is pregnant with the twins and is huge. I am three and I sleep in my own room. I try not to bother her because she needs her sleep but one night, I hear her crying. I get up out of bed and find her in the hall. She bends down and I take her in my arms and comfort her. And then I ask her for a glass of water. I go back to bed and she brings me a glass, placing it on the nightstand. I fall back asleep.

I dream that I knock the glass of water off the nightstand. The water puddles on the floor. I sit up in my bed and look down into the puddle. The pool of water is so clear I can see my face, even in the dark. But it isn't dark anymore. There is light coming from inside the pool. I see my face in the pool and then I see my grandfather's face, the one who died before I was born, whose face I know only from a portrait my grandmother hangs over her TV, replace mine. His face turns from ripples of light into solid face. From his neck, his entire body grows thick in the pool until his feet become as solid as the rest. The light shifts and he steps out of the pool. There is water on his face when he tells me the secret he's been keeping ever since he died. I think he says that he is thirsty.

When I wake up, the glass of water has tipped and spilled onto the floor. All the water has seeped into the carpet. There is no way I can tell this story. I don't have the words yet.

Not Apocryphal

Later, when I did have the words, I told my mom this story; she said no, she wasn't crying because she missed my dad as I had imagined, but that I hadn't been sleeping at all at night. She was exhausted, taking care of me alone, pregnant with twins. It makes me question the power of my comforting self. It makes me question who was thirsty in the night—Grandfather or just me?

Grass

So though I find comfort in the fact that the water that comes from reservoirs merely stops by my toilet, bathtub and sink and will eventually make it back to its original destination, I find no similar comfort in the water I use to keep my lawn green. This water originally streamed nowhere near my backyard. I live on a hill and the canyons' rivers are not particularly close. There is no natural way I'm going to turn my lawn green in this almost-desert land. But there is an unnatural way. I have a maze of sprinklers running through the yard. Reams of PVC, scores of sprinkler heads and something called a Rainbird conspire to bring the water not only to my toilet, but to the sixth of an acre I call my own. I water at least once a week just to keep my grass a tawny green—just enough to give my cats and dog something to chew and lie on. Some of my neighbors have capitulated to the local climate and have rocks and tarpaper for yard. Others water every day, in the middle of the day, not only their grass but their sidewalks too. Both sidewalk and lawn turn an almost mossy blue.

I disapprove of this greening. I spent one summer walking around the neighborhood, handing out conservation brochures my students, in a business writing course, had made. The cover of the brochure pictured a fountain with a boy peeing and the words, "Water Is Life." When you opened it up, it said, "Don't Waste It," on one panel. On the next panel, they had a picture of a fat man bending over to get something out of the fridge. The heading read, "Gluttony: the desire to consume more than what is required," while the bulleted list read:

- The average person needs 4 gallons of water a day to survive.
- The average American uses 190 gallons a day.
- The average Utahn uses 300 gallons a day.

Utahns are always overachieving. I tried to convince my students that the images for the brochure should demonstrate what the text proposed, but, as all things are and should be in the twenty-first century, the gap between the image and the idea is wide. And the inside picture of a man bending over to reach into the bottom of the fridge, revealing his butt crack, demonstrated their point as well.

The brochure listed how much a water user should water his or her lawn, even in the hottest month. Twenty-seven minutes every ten days in July. I drew my highlighting pen over the "every ten days" and stuck the brochure in their fences or on their trees, or, if I was feeling very brave and very criminal, in their mailboxes.

But imagine that even those who over-water, whose lawns look like the mountains of Ireland, where it rains up to eighty inches of rain a year, or the marshes of the Oregon coast, where it rains up to ninety, that the lawn water at least drips down to the aquifer or evaporates to make new clouds or is trapped in the blades of grass to be eaten by cows and goats and deer, then maybe this watering would be akin to flushing.

Except the grass is never eaten by any cud-chewer. The purposeful lawn grower does not wait for the deer to come down the mountain. Goats in cities are fabular. The water doesn't have time to evaporate or drip. The grass imported from Kentucky sucks it up as fast as it can so it can grow tall and be mowed once a week. The clippings go into black Hefty bags which are then tossed in lidded garbage cans. The garbage is picked up also once a week and taken to a landfill. All that water-trapped grass sweats in the bags. Inside the bags, a little swamp begins-—part nitrogen, part water, part cellular shell. Garbage bag is piled upon garbage bag, further trapping the water below. Landfills are lined with plastic for the very purpose of keeping the ground water protected from that which seeps. Landfills are eventually capped. Each swampy Hefty bag makes its own planet. When we run out of water and everyone is thirsty, when the toilet won't flush and the reservoir won't fill, we'll look at that strangely capped landfill, now a brown soccer field, and wonder where those little plastic planets went.

Prison

When I was eight, in our basement lined with bookshelves, I found an old leather bible whose signature page was filled with a long list of names of people I had never heard of. I hadn't seen much of the bible either and was surprised when I found it filed alphabetically by author like the other books. My parents were atheists. They didn't file it under G for God. It was mixed in with the M's, maybe for Moses or Matthew or Mark. Methuselah.

The leather cover, lined with drought, cracked again when I opened it. My mom must have heard it crack. She came down the stairs as if she could smell the desert opening up. She took the book out of my hands. Not too forcefully, but not too gently either. I asked her who those names were. She said Romick was her dad's name. William Ray Romick. They called him Bill. And with that, she pressed the dusty flaps closed and returned the bible to the shelf. Under "P" this time. Higher up on the shelf.

It wasn't until I was in my late teens that I learned anything concrete about him. My great-grandma and grandmother would whisper about Daddy Bill, but they always whispered about everything, so I never knew when I should have listened hard. On one late August day when my mom and Grandma Dee were canning peaches and a storm was moving in, I didn't have to listen hard. They started talking loudly about the house in Evanston. Grandma said that if Bill did nothing else, at least he got my mother and her sisters that house.

No, my mom said, his mother gave us the house. He gave us nothing. He didn't even write us letters. He wrote his mom, but he never wrote us.

Where was he, I asked.

Prison, she said.

For what? I asked.

The air was electric with the coming storm. My hands sticky with peach juice. I waited for her to answer. I wanted her to tell me the whole story. She told me this.

For being a drunk, she answered.

I still don't know exactly why he was there. Even after I read his letters, I only get a sense of what he did. Drinking or robbery. The Korean War has just started and he's itching to get back into the army. To get away from my grandma and my mom or to make money, I'm not sure. He's down from Evanston in Salt Lake after being told no, they wouldn't enlist him. He wanders past Woolworth's and sees through the window a hat he needs. Or maybe he's getting my mom a chocolate or her new baby sister a rattle. Maybe he does think of them. He has no money but he has big pockets. And these are times that stealing a pack of cigarettes warranted a minimum two-year sentence. Before the jails were full. When even people who knew people went to jail. He had senators write on his behalf to get him out. State senators but senators nonetheless.

Or maybe he just had one too many and ended up in a bar fight over the beer the guy had promised to buy him.

My grandfather addressed his letters to his mom from prison, "Mom, Old Dear." He is more reflective than I would have suspected. Literate. In a letter dated August 24, 1953, he writes:

You know, I think that the past two years, though I've been
cut off from many things that are dear to me, had my freedom
taken away (which I do deserve), life has opened up for me.
Before this I could think only of the pleasures of life that
could be purchased with money; my reading was pretty well
confined to shallow, small and overbearing stuff. I hadn't
bothered looking into some of the very old works of Plato and
such. There is a tremendous difference. I guess that when
one finds that liquor is not the 'great boon,' but the great
curse—then his eyes open to quite a number of things that
before seemed so unnecessary. I must, in all honesty, say this
has done me a lot of good. I haven't written of the harm it has
done (not to me) but to the children, you and to Dee. That is
something that is my fault and mine alone. Wonder how long
(if ever) it will take me to right it. Whew! But it is a big job
ahead. I can only say, I'll do my best.

He is in a jail cell in Huntsville, Texas. He sits on the edge of his cot
with his hands square on his knees. He wears white, white trousers,
white coat, white shirt. His walls are empty. He has put his book
down to his side and listens to the wind pick up. He wonders what
he would be doing if he were out. What *was* he going to do when he
got out? Join the Canadian Army? Go back to Evanston and find a
job drilling oil? It's his birthday and he asks, "32, not much to show
for that many years, have I?" But he has three kids, a wife, a job, al-
beit with the state correctional facilities. I'm 32 and have none of
those things. And he wrote sentences like this.

Lady, do you remember the electrical storms that we used to
have in North Platte? I wish that you could have seen the one
here the night of the 12th. I've seen lightning in most of its
most violent forms and in nearly continuous action. Never
have I seen lightning flash so brilliantly or continuously. The
lights were out for a time and I'll swear that I could read a
paper in the flashes and never lose my place from not being
able to see the print. It was the tail end of the storm that hit

Waco . . . and those people really suffered, both there and
at San Angelo, although San Angelo wasn't as hard hit as
Waco. Me, I'm mighty thankful that I was not mixed up in
the storm.

Well, my dear, the old heart beats a bit stronger and freer
tonight, thanks to you. I've got the old hat strapped down and
the fingers crossed.

Wm. T "Bill" Moore, State Senator, wrote to him: "I sincerely would
like to help you as I believe you would never cause society any more
trouble." Those were optimistic times.

Bird Refuge. Bird Refuse.

Wetlands are the filters of our rivers and streams. They are the
sponges that sop up all our effluent. The wastewater from the treatment plants, the run-off from steel plants, the seepage from nuclear
plants. They grow the plants for the plants. Picture reeds, under-
pants and car parts and steel rods strung from them like lice in a
comb. Except they gather the residual from the pants, the parts and
the rods. Stuff you can't see.

Still, birds love these reeds. Outside of Salt Lake City, before the
Bear River purges itself into the Great Salt Lake, it sifts through
the Bear River Bird Refuge. Water pipers, warblers, meadowlarks,
red winged blackbirds, goldeneyes, pintails, bald eagles, great blue
herons, plovers and sandpipers swing by on their way north or their
way south. They nibble some brine shrimp. They preen. They meet
in the middle of a shallow pond and touch beaks, flap wings, challenge each other to a bird dance. Some mate for life. Most, just for
the weekend.

Like most wetlands, the bird refuge sits at a particular low point
in Utah's geography. Like most bodies of water, wetlands move. Although they may seem stagnant, a current of fresh water moves
through the ponds—adding oxygen to keep the algae down and/or
aerate the brine shrimp. But its slow-moving ways let the waste set-

tle or float. The birds pick it up on their feet or in their mouths. Better than water, they move what the water wouldn't carry any further, to the far ends of Canada and Mexico. A little bit of Utah is always being shat across the globe.

The Watertrough

A little before the bird refuge sits the city of Ogden, step-sister of Salt Lake. Where people imagine Salt Lake to be clean and peaceful, Ogden's image, if it has one, is to be the town where the Chinese and the Irish sank the last tie of the Union Pacific and then went downtown to build saloons and fight about who had done the most work.

My grandfather gets out of prison and drives straight to where my grandmother works—the only grocery store in Evanston. He kisses her and asks how are the kids and can he have a little money. She, knowing full well what he'll do with the money, doesn't give him any. So he leaves. He hitches a ride eighty miles down I-80N, heading straight for the lake and then making an abrupt right into downtown Ogden, to stop in the watering hole he knows there. The truck-driver drops my grandfather off at an exit and gets back on the highway. My grandfather walks down the overpass, hails a cab, and asks the cabbie to take him to 25th Street.

On 25th Street my grandfather gets out of the car, reaches into his pockets, leans back into the cab and asks the driver for his money. He has a knife in his hand. The cabbie gives him what he's got and my grandfather flies as though he has wings into the bar for his long-awaited—more than two years—his long-awaited drink.

He is sipping his whiskey when the cops come in. In the darkness of the bar, with its dark wood and two lamps, he squints through the haze—the haze of the cigarette smoke, the haze as the drink hits him hard after two years without, the haze of trying to forget how shitty he felt taking that cabbie's money with a stupid three-inch blade he never would have used anyway.

He stands up when he realizes that it is him that they are talking to. The cops are here already and he hasn't ordered his second drink. They ask him to put his knife down but he has no knife to put down. He has already dropped it on the street on the way in. The police ask him again nicely to drop it. He reaches in his pocket for something—a picture of his daughters, a tissue, the cabbie's money minus the cost of a couple of whiskeys, a senator's note—all the detritus that defines him. He reaches and they shoot. They shoot him in the bottom of his chest, toward the front of the bar in the middle of the day. They couldn't have known all he came for was a pure drink and he couldn't have known that the pure drink he was looking for was the poison that would kill him, one way or another.

Thistle Landslide

What has the power to reshape? Outside sources usually—backhoes and Big Macs, concrete and liposuction, but what can change topography from the inside?

For instance: A hernia is a weakness in the wall of the abdomen. Some hernias are present from birth while others develop later in life, often as a result of persistent straining. Hernias tend to occur at places where there is a natural weakness in the wall of the abdomen, such as in the groin—called inguinal hernias. Hernias occur in both men and women, although inguinal hernias are much more common in men.

Another example of change made from the inside: The Thistle landslide began moving in the spring of 1983 in response to groundwater buildup from heavy rains the previous September and the melting of deep snowpack for the winter of 1982–83. The ground became saturated with water, destabilizing rock and dirt from underneath. Within a few weeks the landslide dammed the Spanish Fork River, obliterating U.S. Highway 6 and the main line of the Denver and Rio Grande Western Railroad. The town of Thistle was inundated under the floodwaters rising behind the landslide dam. Total costs (direct and indirect) incurred by this landslide exceeded $400 million, the most costly single landslide event in U.S. history.

Cause: When I was three my twin sisters were born. Apparently, in a moment of iconographic cuteness, I asked my grandmother when I found out they were twins, "Why so many?" Indeed. Many times my mom and dad must have asked themselves that same question. I can't imagine how they changed two sets of diapers, or how either parent slept when one twin would fall asleep just as the other woke up, or how they kept track of how many bites of applesauce each one ate. I always imagined my mother breastfeeding both of them at the same time. She said she did, once in awhile. But unlike the image in my head of two babies cradled in her arms, crossing her chest, she showed me how she held them: heads in hands, elbows wide to her side, feet pointed outward—it's called the football position. My mom must have felt like a tapped keg—set 'em up, she would say, and the twins would drain her double D's down to a deflated C like football players who drain their forties on Friday nights.

I did, however, after my initial surprise, adapt to their twinness quickly. When my mom wants to let me know how much she appreciates me, she reminds me of how I'd run and get their bottles or find them a blanket. I thought the twins were super fun dolls. I liked to hold them—in the cute way, with their feet crossing in front of me, their heads in the crook of my elbows like koalas in the crotch of bamboo.

When they were older, I started to carry them everywhere. Even more koala-esque—I carried one little twin in my arms and let one climb onto my back. We'd go up the stairs and down the stairs, outside into the backyard and up the rock path my dad built to the garden, and down the deck stairs and across the street to where my mom played bridge and where she would tell me to put them down for once. They were old enough to walk. I was going to break my back. But I loved doing it. I loved that they loved it. I played favorites, alternating daily, letting the best one of the day—the one who smiled at me the most, or made the best joke, or gave me half of her peanut butter cup—ride in my arms. I tried to be fair and trade back for front evenly, but that was harder to keep track of than how many bites of applesauce each one ate.

Cause: In 1983 there was a big flood that affected all of northern Utah. A flood that transformed the landscape—even the cityscape. The concrete, manmade roads and bridges buckled and broke as the snow melted and headed toward the Great Salt Lake any way it wanted—channel, riverbed, waterway be damned. Hills came down and rivers overflowed. City Creek, Salt Lake City's main water source, was redirected over ground and around the downtown, to State Street—an eight-lane major thoroughfare. Now, twenty years later, I live right by City Creek and I wonder where the water has gone. It comes down the canyon, runs into the park, and then disappears. How could that same river have possibly ended up in the middle of the road teenagers dragged on Saturday night? In 1983, it was lined with sandbags. People fished from the sidewalks.

One of the few places permanently affected by the landslide was Thistle, Utah. Thistle, in the first place, was already practically ghostly by 1983. As a railroad town it had ebbed and flowed with Union Pacific's tides. The apex of its population stood at 600 people in the early 1900s. By the time the landslide hit, Union Pacific was mostly happy to find a way out of the money-losing line. As the speed of locomotives had increased, the need for stopovers and refills in small depot towns had lessened. By 1983, only fifty people called Thistle home.

Symptom: I was showering in my mom and dad's bathroom when my mom opened the shower curtain to hand me a washcloth and noticed the lump. She asked how long it had been there. I did not like her looking at my vagina. I told her as much. But she kept looking anyway. I told her I was OK and showed her my neat trick. If you pushed on the lump, it went away. I thought she would like that—it was a little like ironing—press it down and the protruding wrinkle goes away. She did not like it. She called the doctor.

Symptom: For awhile, those floods transformed the riverbeds and the canyon floors, but the most dramatic changes came from underneath. As the water sopped into the sandy ground far above in the mountains, the underlying valley aquifers began to fill. The aquifer just above Thistle filled to the brim and then it bubbled over like any lid that tries too hard to hold the contents of its burgeoning cup. The land that capped the groundwater spectacularly split from the under-lying ground and steamed right in to the town of Thistle. Thistle—dry, pokey, brittle. Nothing wet about it. Not usually. Not until 1983 when the rules changed and the lid was no longer tight enough and the cup no longer big enough and the whole side of the mountain shifted its weight up and over and then down on the town of Thistle.

How literally can you take the metaphor between land and the body? My body houses a number of species of mite and yeast and bacte-rium, and occasionally another human body. A chemical imbalance of any sort can disrupt that number, but even if I manage to kill all the mites off of *my* eyelashes, if they were to go extinct all over *me*, six billion other human-planets would continue to sustain the very same species of mite. The earth, though it may have six billion other brothers and sisters in the universe, as far as we know, is the only one to house anywhere from one-and-a-half to six million species on it. See how a body repairs itself. See how a planet does.

Everyone had to look. My dad. The nurses. The doctor. I think my mom even made me show both my grandmas. Such showing in-volved pulling down my pants just far enough that the slit that began my vagina stayed barely hidden behind my pink-for-girl underwear. The doctor poked at my bulge, made it disappear back behind the wall of muscle from which it had escaped. He was surprised. He'd never seen anything like this on an eight-year-old girl. And I was happy. This was something cool—something only boys got. Now maybe I could do something properly boyish and hit a baseball or mow the lawn. And I did eventually mow the lawn for my dad, every week until I went to college.

In Thistle, when it kept raining through May, you knew there was trouble. The railroad tracks had bent and risen before, but now they twisted so much that the trains had stopped. The silence. You couldn't sleep. Your whole life you'd slept in the back room of your three-room house with your dreams sound-tracked to the pump and whine of metal on metal. The struggle of the engine's climb was your struggle to emerge from sleep and catch the open car up to mornin

Now you toss and turn and listen to your sandstone foundation melting like sugar in caramel.

When the toe of the foothill started nudging its way down Billy Mountain and toward the river bed, you weren't surprised so much by its moving but rather by how slowly it did move. When they came to you in the middle of the night and said, Provo's close to your left, Price is close to your right. Take your essentials and go, you looked around your room—you grabbed the two favorite books from *The Great Brain* series and a copper bell your grandpa bought for you at the Bingham Copper Mine's gift store. Your mattress, which had begun, in the last couple of days, to smell like the sea, and your coat, scoured white from pitching sand into sandbags, you left behind. You moved upland and out of the path of the bulging river.

By the time I was admitted to the hospital for my surgery, I was so used to everyone looking at and poking the lump that I ran around practically naked. I decided it was more boy-like to refuse embarrassment. I even took a sort of pride in the bump and the way it could disappear magically like the 'where's my thumb' trick that I could never master. I spent the whole night keeping the nurses up by pressing the "come quick" button and asking for another popsicle. They kept bringing them to me even though it was the middle of the night. When the girl in the bed next to me woke up screaming and the doctors and nurses rushed in and pulled the curtain around her bed for privacy, I remembered thinking as I sucked on my popsicle, what a wuss that girl was. Whether for the screaming or for the need to keep the curtains closed was one and the same thing to me.

After: When the earth split open and out poked a nice new lake to sit behind the big toe of earth that had moved the river bed and your house, they thought, won't that be nice for irrigating these desert farms. Your house, half melted sandstone and half broken beam, sat at the bottom of their new lake and waited for the drought that was sure to come and give at least its ragged rooftop back to god. Later it was determined that the new lake was unstable and they bulldozed the earth-made dam and began work to restore the road that wound up the hill from Spring City.

Three days after the surgery, I came bounding down the stairs as my Aunt Bev came in our front door. "What are you doing up? Shouldn't you be resting?" She looked so shocked by my recklessness. But I felt fine. The stitches itched a little. What did I care? It was my cousin's birthday, they were in town from Las Vegas, and I had people still bringing me popsicles. Now, I could keep my pants on most of the time. Exposed. Reshaped. Dissolving stitches. I did not know what the fuss was about.

Later: The steepness and severity of the Rocky Mountains actually insist that railroads be laid in the path of potential landslides. Where the land has slid before is where the grades are gentlest. The beds roll and undulate, cushioning the heavy steel cars and their heavy coal cargo up and up the thousands of feet that would otherwise require mountain goat or pickaxe. The Rockies are not known for forgiveness or for making it easy to pass through. And their weather is not the weather of the coasts or the plains. It is unpredictable and nonnegotiable. Later, ten years of drought will invite wildfire and beetle infestations, denuding the land of trees more quickly than any logging company. Then two years of wet will soak the land that is no longer made stable by stubborn root. The land can't be held back or kept under. It moves of its own volition. You can build all you want all over its skin. It certainly does not care. It has plans to take it back.

Later: My body had been re-formed. There's a scar that runs just below the top of my pubic hair that I would show any one who asked. It didn't seem odd, them asking. I took the scar as evidence of my uniqueness. And my toughness—I still like to pick my sisters up, both of whom are now taller than me. It made me sad though that the thing that I thought made me most tough—my ability to admit my injury, to show my flaw—actually led to an immodesty that showed what made me girl. Right down to my anatomy. The body, re-formed, had been returned to what it always had been. And the willingness to show off, to prove unafraid of surgery and unconcerned with privacy, did not have the mountainous effect of transforming me into one of the guys.

Slip

The ladder makes its own clatter as it collapses back into itself. The clang is like the sound of steel wheels clanking against steel tracks, a shuffle of cards, a wagon dragged across the sidewalk's even cracks. The sound I heard was not that sound. At first I thought it was the swamp cooler falling through the roof. And then I thought it was the roof caving in on top of the twins' bunk beds. The ceiling had done that before. The twin, I can't remember which one, woke up with drywall and paint in her mouth and eyebrows. She blinked and I told her she looked like the Pillsbury Doughboy which made her cry. The tears made a paste out of the drywall dust.

In their room though, there was still ceiling and no twin anyway; it was the middle of the day. But out that window, I saw the frame of the aluminum ladder. I wasn't tall enough to see out of the window and down so all I could do was look out into the backyard, through the squares of steps, through the links of fence out onto the green cemetery lawns behind the house.

Somewhere between the cemetery and the twins' bedroom, I could hear my mom yell. To get outside, I had to back up through the twins' room, walk down the hall, through the kitchen, through the dining room and out to the back patio. I could have run but the sound I'd heard had been too thudding, too all-stop, too full of gravity.

He was blinking when I got out there. My mom was alternately standing up and pacing and kneeling down to ask him if he was OK, where did it hurt, should she call an ambulance. My dad, not usually such a blinker, usually one who avoids hospitals even if his kid has broken her tooth or her arm, blinked twice at the suggestion for an ambulance. My mom took this for a yes, told me to wait there with him while she went to call 911.

I lay down next to him. I didn't really know what to say. I was eight. I was used to lying in the backyard while we looked up at constellations while he told me which one was which and I pretended to know exactly what he was pointing at, but now I was expected to keep the conversation going, to keep asking him if he was OK, as if stopping would be to let him sleep, or be in pain, or even die. I told him how when he was building the rock wall and I was helping, or pretending to help, by bringing him the occasional rock for the wall, I pretended I was Rapunzel and he was building me a tower. I told him how when he built the wrap-around deck from the front of the house to the back, that I made it into a cruise ship and I was driving the boat to Hawaii, how the walk he built from the lower half of the yard to the garden space above was a yellow brick road and sometimes I was glad to get out of Kansas.

He blinked. I talked about the yard he lay in, pointing out the heavy work and the play work, the green grass, the swamp cooler cover that had been on the roof with him and that now hung from the gutters like a lost balloon.

The Wasatch Fault lines the Salt Lake Valley like a bathtub ring. The ring does faintly describe the edge of what used to be Lake Bonneville. When I drive along the beltline and see the gigantic houses being built as they cling to the mountainside, I imagine the houses popping off the side of the hill as the big quake shakes them loose, sends them tumbling down the hill like they were only boulders.

But this is not what will happen. The houses on the hill, the seismologists say, are relatively secure. It's the houses in the valley, on the flat parts, that are most vulnerable. The valley floor is a deep, sedimentary-filled basin. Tectonic plates have been shifting since at least the Paleozoic era. There are slips and sand, sand and slips. Underneath the clay and sand, in between the clay and sand, sometimes riding on top is the remnant of that old lake. Part aquifer, part memory, the city rolls on the sandy waves of its ancestry. In an earthquake, sand and clay lead to liquefaction of the valley floor. Buildings don't tolerate this well. The ground shakes, the sand settles. Water runs between cracks. The ground oscillates. Oscillations make waves. The ground packs and bends and slides until the trapdoor that was pretending to be a solid building foundation falls open and the building slips through the stage floor.

I am twelve and after four years of occasional pain, my dad has finally had the disk that slipped when he fell from the roof operated on. He is in bed for a month. He can't walk except for short jaunts to the bathroom. My mom and my sisters and I take him lunch and quickly turn to close the door on the room where the blinds are shut and the dad lies down and the neck brace taunts. His legs wither.

My dad, protector via technology more than weapon or brute force, has an alarm system installed on the doors of the house. While he's incapacitated, we will be able to deflect burglars and detect fires. As if, when he was well, he stood guard at night. As if his nose could smell the smoke of mis-wired circuit panel. As if his very ability to stand upright kept danger at bay.

Then I am thirteen, and this alarm system runs counter to my attempts to be the baddest thirteen-year-old of the neighborhood. My friends, who were in high school and better versed in badness, snuck out of their houses at night. If I wanted to be bad and if I wanted to be of high school bad caliber, I had to make it out of the house after midnight. Two touchpads turned the alarm off and on—one by the garage door, one in my parents' bedroom closet. My parents armed the alarm at night when they went to bed. The sound of the secret code being punched in—38, 38, my parents' age at the time—chimed through the whole house. If you beeped the one by the garage, the touchpad in their room would echo the beeps. Motion detectors guarded every door to the outside. None of the windows that opened were at street level. I was as good as trapped.

Except. Except there was one window off the dining room that opened onto the roof of the hot tub room. I had helped him build the room by bringing him nails and boards. I had watched him make a solid structure where once was air. The furnace for the hot tub stood just outside the newly built room, made just one small jump down onto what became, for me, a kind of ladder. My dad had built the roof I slid out onto. I used the gutter for a hand-hold, jump-stepped onto the furnace, and slipped into the night.

Most of the time, Mark and Linda and I would go sit on the lawn in the dark and pull blades of grass through our teeth, chewing the white bits clean, pretending we were self-sustaining, talking about music, listening to the sound of trains. But sometimes, Linda wouldn't show and Mark and I would find taller, drier grass to lie down in, in the field that would later become a grocery store.

I got caught by my mother, who had sensed something was up. The screen to the window didn't fit like it used to. She asked me what was going on and I told her about Tony who had just wanted to talk to me and had thrown pebbles at my window. He must have thrown a rock right at the screen, I said. I went out and gathered some rocks to scatter on top of the hot tub roof as soon as my mom went to run some errands.

My mom was not that gullible.

The next night when I went to open the dining room window, my mother rose from where she'd been waiting on the neighboring room's couch. My rock story had been unconvincing. I don't remember what she said but I went back up to bed, feeling guilty that my friends were left waiting for me under the streetlight where we'd planned to meet. The next day, the alarm technicians came to install a motion detector on the stairs that led from my second story bedroom to my escape window below. Rapunzeled.

Later, like a year ago, my sisters told me my parents slept hard, at least when they first went to sleep. The twins would just waltz right into our parents' bedroom, duck into the closet where the alarm is, shut the closet door to muffle the sound, and beep their way out of the house. It's one thing to be high school clever. It's another to be as clever as downy, innocent-seeming, younger sisters.

Avalanches aren't downy. Most of them, especially the deadly ones, are dry slab avalanches. Something underneath has gone wrong, shown weakness, a chink in the armor. Snow, lying blanketed on top of a lawn, does a good job of looking like a unified force. It seems like one snowflake matches up nicely with any other, making a bank, a bond, a friendly cohesion. But in the desert mountains, hot days and cold nights let snow melt and refreeze. The new snow just isn't like the old snow and there are bonds that were born to be broken. Or never made. There's a new layer of snow sitting on top of another layer of snow like a Napoleon. There's a between there even though it looks the same—blank canvas, wall of white. It takes some force, more than noise or wind but less than a Cat tracker or snowmobile to nudge that fissure open. Crack open that thin fissure and it's not a blizzard but a building, not a feather gust but a chunk of the Great Wall of China tumbling under you at eighty miles per hour. And since you don't ski, or run, or snowmobile, or fly that fast, you trip into the slab and then you trip under it. The snow falls on you and around you. The snow gets hot from all the friction. You are as much slab as tree and boulder. The whole earth is coming down and you are so connected. The falling stops eventually. Those bonds. They're made now. They're clinched. You have fifteen minutes before someone finds you. Swim. Turn that slab of snow back into water. Breast-stroke your way into transformation. But if you didn't know about the swimming or if you doubt your power to convert solid into liquid, claw a breathing hole, if your arms are free and unbroken. The bigger the hole, the more likely you'll last the entire fifteen minutes. Once those fifteen minutes are up, the snow that was so falling, so moving, so full of friction will pack now and harden and turn to ice. Carbon dioxide can't get out and oxygen can't get in. You are snow. You're into and under and of that thing you were just trying to slide on.

My parents finally got divorced when I was in college. It wasn't so much the drinking, although that did its part. It was the casual ways he'd let slip some of his more common betrayals. He'd left the receipt for some flowers that my mother never received in his pocket. When my mom reconciled some bank statements, she found item lines for two tickets for a trip my mother wasn't invited on. He left a pair of women's cowboy boots, not her size, in the back of his car. Of course he wanted to get caught. Of course he thought he was James Bond or some other chivalrous martini drinker. He didn't see the hands shaking, didn't hear the slurred words, didn't feel the stumblings. And though he'd been a severe but functional alcoholic when he and my mother were together, after she left, he lost his moorings. There was no stopping and no comparison. He couldn't reflect because his mirror of twenty-four years had not even asked for any cowboy boots.

When I came home from college on break, my sisters introduced me to dad-Sundays. Our family had been going to the Oyster Bar since I was thirteen. The first time my sisters tried oysters and liked them, I cringed and asked my dad if we could order another dozen just for me. Until then, I'd shared the dozen with my mom and dad. Four for me. A dozen was hard to divide among five. After the divorce, my dad stopped eating oysters anyway. Now, my sisters and I split the dozen while my dad ordered shrimp cocktail and proceeded to lie down on the bench seat.

This is what he does now, they told me.

He doesn't even finish the shrimp.

He drinks his Bloody Mary and excuses himself to the car. He'll wait for us there. We finish our oysters and down our glasses of wine and wonder whether he's drinking or sleeping in the car.

We drive him home. My sixteen-year-old sisters go in his office to print the checks that pay his bills.

My dad lies down on the couch and starts to shake. Maybe he's not drinking and it's delirium tremens. Maybe it's the ammonia in his blood. Maybe it's the beginning of Korsakoff syndrome but he's trying to tell me something. He's telling me about the time his mother had a bird trapped in the house. She'd opened the back door and the bird flew in. I told her the bird must have been sick, he said. But she went to the bird and picked him up. She set him outside the door. He didn't fly away. A few hours later, my mom went to check, he said. The bird was dead. He told me my grandmother cried and said that it wasn't her fault. It wasn't her fault, he said over and over.

The bird's alive mom, he said, and I said I see it. My dad points at the ceiling that is as smooth and white as snow. I lie down on the couch next to him and pretend to see the starlings.

Water and ground don't mix. Or, when they try to, they mix badly. In an earthquake, liquefaction turns sand into water making a kind of quicksand. On a hill, water undercuts the ground, pulling the rug out. If it snows in the mountains, which is the only way certain valleys can collect any water, then the snow melts according to the rules of gravity. It comes in marked rivers and streams. But it also comes from underneath. Melted snow makes its own streams, new burrows to make it downhill as fast as it can.

There are houses on the hill that are sliding. It's not the sudden break of earthquake or avalanche but the slow slide of a stream running under the ground, inching out the dirt from underneath the concrete foundations. The foundations crack. The porches split off. In a flood year, you can see the dirt move, mud rivers running around and past the house until then you see not just mud but house and mud, the whole house, twisted and wrested from its moorings. The whole house moves whole, down the hill for a minute. And then second stories become first stories, front rooms swallow the kitchens and the mud that held the promise of flat and level and home and safe.

The Weight of a Bird

The weight of a contour feather is not nothing. Smooth and firm. Solid. More like marble than spider webs or pollen or dandelion seed. It takes prying fingers to separate the individual barbules, unknit their hooks, separate the whole vale into wiry hairs. To rub a feather backwards is to undo its featherness. The possibility of its flight is now as likely as that of yours or mine. Even if you slide your hand back up the shaft, smoothing out the barbs, they don't reweave properly—now you've turned a crane into an emu.

A boy I know little about climbed the fence that bordered Tracy Aviary in Liberty Park. The sole of his shoe left marks like chalk against the brick wall. Nothing else took note of the scaling or the wall, not the circling security guards, not the sleeping birds. Brick is easy to scale, the wall was very silent, and he was very fast.

Did he choose the flamingo because it was the first bird he saw or the first to awaken? Did he choose it because the bird was closest to the boy's height or that its pink feathers were as close to the color of his skin as any bird there? Or was it the bird's utter difference— the plunging of his hands between feathers that was not hair. The reedy, fleshless legs. Its monomorphic genitals—the not knowing whether it was a boy bird or a girl bird he was opening? Did the walnuty cleft dissolve when he touched it? Did he stroke the bird's head or its cottony neck? Did the bird try to fly as the boy came inside it? Did his wings stretch toward the tree branches, over the gate, past the telephone wires? Or was that great lifting done by the boy— the bird light as dust in his hands, the bird pinned into itself, barb crossing barb, leg crossing leg, the bird closing at the boy's insistent opening? Were his wings already clipped or was this the last night she knew how to fly?

~ ~ ~

I do not like the way the words I love you hollow out the air around you. How sometimes, when you hear those words, you think of pickles or stubbed toes or the time your dad was late to pick you up from practice, but don't think about the person saying the words. I love you as a placeholder for all the things you used to know like the smell of dirt as dirt, the smell of fire as fire. The letter U at the end of the phrase leaves you off at the place where you turn toward metaphor. When you say I love you, you might as well say I love the sky, the wind, the water. Your flight. I love you keeps you pinned here.

~ ~ ~

Tracy Aviary is in the middle of the city park. The park is half a mile long and a quarter mile wide. They have boat shows on the lawns. Family reunions, which, in Utah, can number, both in terms of how many individual reunions held each year and in terms of how many participants, into the hundreds, settle into every pavilion. There's a carousel and a big pond on which you can take out paddleboats. It's like a small Central Park, but simultaneously less classy and less seedy. Sometimes the carousel works, sometimes it doesn't. Sometimes the pond is drained of water. But the Aviary is always there and open daily. Even in the winter. Some of the birds there are native— the red-tailed hawks, turkey vultures, golden and bald eagles. The geese and ducks. Even the swans, who at least twice a year migrate through the wetlands off of the Great Salt Lake.

But there are some true aliens there. Emu and scarlet ibis, toucan and flamingo.

After everything came out, my mom told me the neighbors had said I'd seduced their son. They'd found Playboys scattered across their backyard. They said I must have done it. I imagined them waking up, taking their coffee outside, and looking down from their deck onto what should have been green grass but instead was fleshy pink rounds of women, staring back up at them. Maybe it was another neighborhood girl. Maybe it was his sister. Maybe even, after it all, my dad had become fed up with it all and dragged his boxes of Playboys out of the attic, hauled them down the street and plastered them onto their lawn. I said it hadn't been me. But at this point, no one was believing me anymore.

~ ~ ~

Sometimes, I picture my friends who live in other cities. I picture other city streets and my friends walking along them. I impose myself in those pictures. Fogged street lamps. Rain falling horizontally. Cities with hydrangeas and rhododendrons. With wrought iron rings sticking out of the sidewalk to hook your horse to. The space between where I was, hot, sand, desert, and where I thought I should be, wet, floral, heavy, was slippery. I cast my anchor far and deep but could never find my purchase. The area below me filled with gravity. Gravity made me cry. I longed for moving trucks and waterways that bulged big enough to transgress dams, to make it out to sea.

~ ~ ~

Emus, like flamingoes, have long necks and legs. The similarities seem to end there. The flamingo flies. The emu does not. But it's not weight that keeps the emu earthbound. It's its feathers. Each feather has two shafts, with barbs so widely spaced that they do not interlock to form firm vanes as they do in most birds; instead they form a loose, hair-like body covering. Feathers, un-barbed, cannot lie down. They cannot streamline. They cannot loft. They're less than a tenth the length of the emu's body. He's more bone and skin than bird. His feathers pillow and puff. They cotton out. Stick your head deep in the duff of emu feather. His feathers will tickle your nose and your ears but his wings will not contour.

The emu as chameleon. The emu barbless. The emu without a sex until she is reproductive.

~ ~ ~

Every girl knows that when the blood stops, the something else has begun. He asked me as we sat by each other on the piano stool. It was the closest we'd ever appeared in public. It was the closest our bodies had ever been outside of either the basement, or, when I had sleepovers at his sister's, his room. He was an ugly guy. I didn't like seeing him with so much light. Blackheads on his bulbous nose, Brillo-pad hair. No, that's not true. I did like seeing him. He was older. Cooler. I wanted to be his girlfriend but he had started driving and now brought other girls home from church. He was working on getting a girlfriend. Such work had nothing to do with me. I did like seeing him up close. Because he sat beside me so closely I thought that meant something. Because he whispered in my ear everything will be OK, I, beautifully, thought it would be.

~ ~ ~

I used to think that things connected like trains. One boxcar coupled to another and then those thoughts and ideas would add up to mean something. One long train like a strand of DNA would translate to something. I started at this station and I ended up at this next one via this ton of metal, this axle, this track brought me from here to there. Now I think connections are more like Virginia Creeper or spaghetti. It all touches, but where one vine or strand begins and another ends is a knotted question.

~ ~ ~

I spend what I think is an inordinate amount of time trying to fake myself out. Reverse-psychology fate. I tell myself there is no mail with good news, that there is no phone call with the job, that the drought will last forever, that damming the free-running Bear River is a good thing. It's the opposite. I so believe that there will be good news in the mail, a job on the phone, that today is the day it will rain, that democracy rules the world. I have to guard against disappointment. Sometimes I get confused though and don't remember what it is I want. Maybe I don't really want a job. Maybe I like the sun and the parched ground. Maybe I like lakes over rivers.

~ ~ ~

The night after it started—not the night he babysat, but the next night, when I'd recovered from the surprise, when instead of feeling embarrassed and heavy, I felt light and womanly. I could hack this, I figured. We played truth or dare. His sister went to bed. We stayed outside. Truth, he answered. Do you love me? I wanted to ask. Instead, I asked, who was the first person you kissed? Dare, I answered. Take off your shirt. Dare, he answered. I dared him to tell me who, besides his family, first saw him all the way naked. Truth, I said. Dare. I dared him to run inside and steal a beer. He shook his head and told me to take a dare. Show me the pinkest part of you. I opened my mouth to show him my tonsils. His eyes ignored my face. His hands followed the trace my finger had left. He left my clothes outside and had me lie down on an old mattress in the basement. His fingers felt more like barbs than feathers. I scooted around until the barbs stopped. I tried to smile. I tried to make my face look like the face of a happy lover. Like a Playboy bunny. Like a beautiful bird, on the edge of a lake, waiting for the air that would lift me up. By the time I got the smile on, he had stopped lying on top of me. He told me I better go. Outside, I got dressed.

MAN SEES SALT LAKE AS FLAMINGO HAVEN
CATHERINE S. BLAKE
Associated Press

SALTAIR, Utah—Long-legged, pink flamingo seeking same to share friendship, food and freedom. That's the personal classified ad that a lonely flamingo living on the Great Salt Lake may have been thinking about for the last 15 years, said Jim Platt, who has made it his mission to acquire friends for the bird, nicknamed "Pink Floyd."

Since Floyd flew the coop from Salt Lake City's Tracy Aviary, he's been gloriously free, but painfully alone.

His only pals are a pack of seagulls and the tourists who snap his picture. Floyd has become a local legend, appearing frequently in winter as a flash of pink on the otherwise drab horizons of the lake.

"I know what freedom is, and I think Floyd is having that experience," Platt said. "I'd like him to be friends with others who are having that same experience. They could breed and be a wild flock."

Platt, the owner of Dancing Cranes Imports, offered to buy—and release—the remaining flamingos from the aviary for $1,000 each but he was politely turned down. The aviary called the proposition irresponsible and potentially disruptive to the lake's delicate ecosystem.

"If we could look at having some guarantees that flamingos would not procreate out there, then we might be more amenable to the idea," he said.

"But the idea of releasing any wildlife that is not native to the area is courting ecological disaster. We don't want the Great Salt Lake to be a proving ground for that."

Environmentalists cite pigeons, starlings and sparrows—nonnative species that have become pests around the lake.

Because Floyd's gender is not known, releasing birds of either gender isn't practical, said Patty Shreve, Tracy Aviary curator. And it's difficult to neuter birds. She stressed that a flamingo flock would overwhelm the natural environment.

—Copyright © 2011 by The Associated Press

~ ~ ~

Things that don't fit: clothes, squares in round holes, atheists, rain in Utah, interrogative sentences, the letter U, steam engines, buffalo, dare without truth, wine at a pub, the color pink in nature, the idea that what you believe affects the outcome of events.

~ ~ ~

Pink stands on one leg and then the other. It is winter and he has most of the brine shrimp to himself. The algae in the lake keep the shrimp pink, which in turn, keep Pink's feathers pink. He looks around at the intermittently arriving birds. Snowy plovers, seagulls, the occasional Tundra Swan. Their white, white coats match the falling snow. As far as Pink can see, snow covers lake and reed and mountain. Even the sky is heavy with white snow. His feathers are a target. His feathers are fleshy, open, obvious. Out there. No one who drives by would miss him. They might roll their eyes, wondering why he hasn't taken off to Chile with the rest of his flock. His beak scratches at his underwing. He stands alternately on one foot, and then the other. He looks around at the white plumage of the other birds. He plucks a pink feather. He plucks another.

Easy

In August under a full moon, I could hike all the way up to Lake Catherine in the dark. Three miles over rocks and pot guts (ground squirrels to the non-Utahn) I stepped on what I would know to be, in daylight, years later, evening primrose and feverfew. It was a steep hike, but at fourteen years old with mostly pink lungs and some motivational strychnine-laced LSD, I walked fast. We would make it up in time, as long as we stayed focused on our destination.

On our hike up to the lakes, I try to convince David and Mark, who weren't skiers, that I could pinpoint trails and trees that I had skied past last winter. What turned out to be the last winter I would ski for almost five years since they didn't ski and I lacked the foresight or the fortitude to go on my own. Or with my dad. Or with girlfriends. I'd skied there every winter weekend since I was five but, the truth was, without the snow, in the dark, nothing looked familiar. I thought I saw a cabin I knew hidden in the pine trees, what would have been halfway down the run, but I wasn't sure how many cabins dotted the ski runs. I'd never thought of the people living there. Instead, I thought about how, in the deep winter, before either Mark or David was my boyfriend, I fantasized a blizzard kicked up and I took one more run while my dad headed back to the lodge. Blinded by snow, I tried to make it to the cabin. Inside, a ski patrolman is already there. He takes my hands and warms them up in his. We sit by the fire as he kisses me.

Now, though, the cabin of my dreams looks inhabited by people from the city. There's a Jeep halfway up the mountain in what I had thought was an isolated and remote area. Now, as I follow the track of the Jeep's tires, I can see a well-traveled road. But by the time we reach Mary's lake, there are no more cabins. Only a row of chairlift poles implies manmade. By the time we reach Catherine, there's not even a sign of a chairlift.

Lake Mary and Lake Catherine are both made from and surrounded by shale rock. There are only two formations of shale rock in the United States. One is in Wyoming, the other stretches from the Uintas to the Green River. Shale is unique sedimentary rock because it's full of kerogen. Kerogen is water and peat and fish and algae, pressed into the sand, millions of years ago. Now, that dry ground underneath makes a bed for a lake with water as clear as sky. The shale rock is as visible a hundred feet under the surface as it is by you as you try to sit on a slice of it and it breaks under your butt and you think, what kind of rock is this? Weak. Flaky. Malleable.

The shale, rich in substance, makes the oil industry salivate. What promises fuel underground in seeps and wells is promised by shale. Pressure often leads to something good. The oil companies have already tried to squeeze oil out of the shale in Wyoming and the Uintas. They haven't started on Big Cottonwood just yet.

You're not supposed to swim in the lake. It's too cold. It's a watershed. In the day, you can see the pink of the bank as it slides into the blue of the water. By the time we got to the top, I was hot. You're not supposed to swim here but I'm having a hard time knowing which rules to actually follow and which rules to break. And Mark and David were telling me about the time they came up and slept over and saw an albatross, which would have been a rare sight indeed. They always made me feel jealous and like I was a nuisance because I couldn't go camping. My parents let me date David, who is three years older than me, as long as I got good grades. Midnight was my curfew. It was already nine and dark in the mountains. I could barely see the bottom of the lake. I couldn't see any albatrosses.

I didn't want to get into a debate over whether albatross existed in Salt Lake. Seagulls whiten every shore of the Great Salt Lake and many parking lots, but albatross only inhabit the southern hemisphere, like the Southern Cross. Maybe Lake Catherine is so deep that her source is New Zealand. Maybe there's some earthly wormhole and the cool, almost winter nights of the high altitude icy water draws the albatross straight through. Or maybe they had taken a lot more LSD that time and had been listening to PIL's "Albatross" too often. Sometimes, when you take too much LSD, you forget the rules of the universe.

It was hot.

I took off my clothes and jumped into the water. I would rather look sexy than like a know-it-all and I was about to explain the territorial patterns of the albatross. The water was cold. Cold that constricted your ribs. Mark and David pointed out the rock they had jumped from last summer. In the daytime. When the sun would have a chance to warm them when they got out. They started arguing about which rock it had been. They had to reenact the entire previous trip. They were just stalling for time. But if they didn't get in soon, I'd have to get out. This water was colder than my imaginary blizzard.

I kicked my legs. The moon was strong enough, or close enough that high up the Wasatch, that I could see my legs under the water. Just water and rocks and skin. I didn't mind being naked. I'd dated Mark right before David. All my secrets had been exposed to each of them, or both of them. I felt invisible, down in the lake with both of them tall and sure-footed on dry land as they stumbled over huge boulders, trying to pick just the right one. One would run to a rock and claim it was the one they had jumped from before. The one they had lain on top of when they saw the albatross. Then the other would say no, this one. They made it all the way around the lake, potential rock by potential rock, without taking off a shred of clothes. By the time they got back to where I'd jumped in, I'd almost turned glacial. I felt white and dumb under the light, in the freezing water. I hated them to see me cold but they weren't seeing me at all. My need to beat them to the water, my ability to get so naked so fast, the fact I had to get out and hike home now before midnight all seemed so obvious.

Oil shale is mined the usual way that the valued mineral is divested of the unvalued rock—strip mining or open pit mining. By blowing the less useful, lighter rock away, the heavy stuff you were looking for reveals itself to you like the gift it truly is. The dumptrucks cart the useless dirt away, you haul the shale in felt-lined boxcars. The kerogen is like a little secret, best tucked away in the dark, stored in a metal warehouse until you have the skill to squeeze its usefulness out.

Back when I was going out with Mark, before I started dating David, we went windsurfing. He picked me up in his 1967 Microbus, put in the windsurfer he won by cashing in his Camel Bucks, and we drove out to Stansbury Lake—a small fresh water reservoir next door to the briny Great Lake, established mostly to keep the nearby golf course green.

We drove out to the lake, shooed away brine shrimp, ate buckets of sunflower seeds and smoked Camel cigarettes on the beach, occasionally bothering to put out the smoke to venture into the tiny lake. The sail for the windsurfer weighed more than the board itself. I could bring the sail up if it pointed straight down but if the sail fell sideways and took on water, Mark had to swim out to pull the sail up for me. We didn't last long at the lake. By the time we got home, Mark was tired of hanging out with me. He and David took off for Lake Mary. Their parents didn't mind them sleeping over night, anywhere.

There are ways around all rules, even those that seem like they're set in stone. That following winter, a friend of Mark's gave him a key to a cabin. It's a rare thing, for a sixteen-year-old boy to have a key to a house all for himself. He could have chosen to have a party up the canyon. He could have had David and a bunch of guys and me too, but he asked if I could come.

I wanted to make him happy. I wanted to go. I wanted to be the grown up with a special night in a special cabin up the mountain where we'd been last summer, hiking outside.

I told my mom I was sleeping over at Shannon's. What a cliché of an excuse—spurious because I hadn't seen Shannon in years. It got me out of the house with many promises that I wasn't lying. My mom reminded about my special privileges—that I got to stay out until ten on weeknights and midnight on weekends as long as I got good grades and came home on time. I promised. I'm going to Shannon's. And Mom hadn't had, in awhile, a reason not to believe me. She dropped me off at Shannon's house. Shannon, covering for me, let me in and let me right back out again when Mark pulled into the driveway an hour later.

When Mark and I made it to Brighton, we parked the car in the ski lot. Most of the skiers had left for the day and there were just a few lights burning through the snow as it fell. Our directions were to walk back toward the Big Cottonwood Canyon Road from the parking lot. We looked for a little red A-frame with a blue door. The snow was piling in my hair like a hat. Mark brushed it off, kissed my wet head. We kept walking. We went down the road until there were no more cabins. We walked back toward the parking lot and then down again. We even tried the key in a red cabin with a green door, but that wasn't the one. We walked and walked under the falling snow. What had been two people looking for a romantic wonderland walking became two people, out of place, looking for something they shouldn't have, desperate and cold.

Mark took me home. When I walked in, I was prepared for a story about how Shannon had gotten sick but when I looked at my mom's face I knew she knew.

Her forgiveness worked like this: she made Mark and me tacos even though it was past ten o'clock. She sat with us while we ate and brought more cheese over when we ran out. But just as Mark stood to go, she stopped Mark, touched his shoulder and said, "It took me a long time to trust you. I trusted you guys." Mark was wounded. He loved my mom. But unlike Mark, I got the guilt plus a grounding. I had to stay home for two weeks and wouldn't be allowed to pretend to sleep over at Shannon's, or anyone's, again.

Geologic information: Oolitic sand is an unusual sediment that is found in and around the Great Salt Lake. Instead of forming from grains of mineral fragments washed down from higher ground, this sand formed within the Great Salt Lake. It is composed of tiny, light-brown, rounded oolites.

An oolite has a shell of concentric layers of calcium carbonate that precipitated around a nucleus or central core. The nucleus is usually a tiny brine shrimp fecal pellet or a mineral fragment. Oolites form in shallow, wave-agitated water, rolling along the lake bottom and gradually accumulating more and more layers.
www.geology.utah.gov/utahgeo/rockmineral/collecting/ oolitic.htm

Which would you rather be? A grain of sand made by erosion? Years and years of wind and water wearing you down? Or would you rather be built up from layers of brine shrimp poop? The latter may be more disgusting but you are growing bigger rather than shrinking into oblivion. To grow from something gross suggests a rare ability to overcome your circumstances.

Rare stuff is useful. It's not only a surprise and a joy because it distinguishes itself from everything else around it. Because it's not usual, it's automatically valuable. Nights away at cabins, windsurfers brought to you by Camel Bucks, kerogen inside of shale rock. It's all so much better because it was hard to get. But not always does the rare thing provide what you hope. Sometimes you end up grounded, with incipient lung cancer, and the detritus left behind from shocking rock for oil.

Twenty years later, I found out that the lakes up Big Cottonwood Canyon were man-made. A 1917 water project built the dams that made Lake Mary and Lake Catherine. That kind of news reshapes memory just as it reshapes the topography on which you stand. These were precious lakes. And yet now they somehow seemed false—full of bad reality. That kind of news shocks like jumping into those cold lakes shocks. But at least that jumping-into-cold-shock, recorded bodily, was real.

Now when I head up the canyon, I look at the landscape differently. Those boulders that lay at the bottom of the bowl that makes the ski runs didn't just fall there. They were hauled over. Stacked. The lakes under the snow had been a puddle that rose barely as deep as I was tall, let alone as far as through to New Zealand. Or even the water table. The lakes had been engineered to serve the greater Salt Lake Valley with a reliable drinking water source and let the farmers irrigate their crops from pumped water rather than pumping their own water from creeks and canals that naturally ran by their land. The creeks would be diverted. They'd make one large pot of water that everyone could feed off. The farmers irrigated. The city dropped water and sewer lines. Salt Lake Valley, the mostly arid flatland that once held a lake so large it could have almost been an ocean, now piped as much water from mountain streams and lakes to make a small lake in everyone's bath, sink, toilet and trough.

It is not easy to bend nature to your will. It is not easy to extract oil from shale. The process, pyrolysis, takes heat and the removal of oxygen to convert the kerogen into synthetic oil. Sometimes, pyrolysis is done on site if there's a reliable energy source around to make the heat and absent the oxygen. Sometimes, you haul the kerogen off in box cars or semi-trucks. Either way, it takes a lot of energy to get any potential oil out of the rock and you never know exactly how much quality kerogen is lurking in your useless silt, but you press the button anyway. Add heat and pressure. You pray to see liquid dripping from stone. You're a little disappointed when you only get thirty tons of oil per hour. Your goal had been forty, but you shrug your shoulders, add a bit more heat to the coke. You take what you can get and leave the extraneous sulfates, heavy metals, polycylic aromatic hydrocarbons behind.

Lake Bonneville had supported dinosaurs and ancient flora which is why they look to extract oil in Utah—either from its easier ground or harder rock. People get excited about extracting oil from shale as if somehow that oil would burn more preciously. As if the shale oil, combusting in that engine, would propel the car forward further or at least more smoothly. But shale oil burns just as fast as oil gotten any other way.

Mark and I broke up the next spring. I had called him to see when he was picking me up, if he would be there by five. I wanted to know if he was coming over to dinner. My mom was making tacos. But his mom answered the phone instead of him. She didn't know where he was but she knew he'd taken his sleeping bag. I asked if David had gone with him. No, she said. David's right here. He was looking for Mark too.

I hung up. I called back later. The phone just rang and rang.

The next day, Mark came by in his Microbus. He told me he was selling it to David. He was buying a new car.

Where were you last night? I thought you were coming over. My mom made tacos.

I went camping up Tanner's. I had to think.

You went camping alone?

With Karen, he answered.

It is not so hard to break the rules.

Bonneville Lake was a rare inland sea. The remnants of the lake can still be found. Bone fossils in eastern Utah. A watery fossil in the form of the Great Salt Lake in the west. The Great Salt Lake is the end of the line for the mountain rivers and for the sewer and storm drains. This rare position doesn't necessarily make it a diamond in the rough. In fact, the Great Salt Lake has been roughed up further because it's so odd and yet so seemingly without value. Only brine shrimp and brine flies find sustenance in that briny water.

What happens to rare things that are not useful? A causeway divides the lake making it saltier on one side than the other. Industries send their dump trucks to drive their tailings out toward Antelope Island and then to drive home toxin-free. The lake is shallower now because waste fills the lakebeds and drought means the water doesn't reach the lake. One day, with enough drought, even the shallow spread of water that goes on for a hundred square miles will be gone. It will become clear that things are not where they should be: little lakes in the mountains, cabins in the middle of ski runs, cigarette-smoking girls on the beach, oil seeping out of rocks. We'll look at the desiccated ground, if we're still here, and think this lake used to be a natural thing, but now it is only salt and salt isn't that hard to find.

Transubstantiation

Transformation is a two part process: a combination of substitution and disappearance. The first element, the original, on its way to becoming something else, is no longer itself. The new element fully replaces the first. The first element: you can't find it anywhere.

Imagine a planet thick with ferns, with trees that grew sideways, where moss hung to the floor. Picture great seas of rain hooking ground cover to canopy. A wall rug of green. Imagine this place is neither the Pacific Northwest nor the Amazon. Imagine that between the drops of rain and connecting flora, gigantic eyes peer. So much water makes everything gigantic: trees, eyes, scales, legs, tails, sloths. Were the carbon atoms themselves larger then? Could you, if humans existed then, hold one in your hand and look at each of the eight electrons? Carbon, like water, connects. Its atoms are strangely able to bond with themselves, making them strong. They're also willing to bond to many other elements, particularly hydrogen, oxygen, nitrogen and the halogens, making them kind of slutty with their willingness to interact with almost anyone.

Coal is one allotrope of carbon. In the diamond structure, each carbon atom is covalently bonded to four others and has a tetrahedal geometry. In essence, a diamond is one large molecule. And yet, what can you really know about elemental essence? Is the carbon in a piece of black coal still coal inside the diamond? Is a fiddlehead's frond, crushed by millennia, a watery diamond or a molecule of thick water, still a frond? First forms are more morphing than they are constant, more like open bonds outstretched like arms always reaching to slide into or onto something, always willing to change into something else.

~ ~ ~

There was a snake lying across one of the lanes of the four-lane road that connected to the city's suburbs via only dirt and rock. The four-lane's beginning was nothing but scrub oak and, apparently, snake habitat. The end was the edge of the foothills, the end of the city, the beginning of orchards and horses. A road that wound, snakelike, and then disappeared into some pastoral landscape we pretended had something to do with nature but was really irrigated farmland.

There wasn't much we could do for the snake—Mark's Volkswagen Fastback had run right over it. Mark got out to look at it. The thing was flattened in two parts. The blood is dry, Mark called as he bent over the snake, looking at the tires of his car and then back to what was left of the body. Some heavier automobile had already pressed most of this snake into the ground, tucking its energy into the dirt for future generations' resource needs. I didn't kill it, Mark noted happily. He liked animals—even snakes. He was glad he hadn't hurt anything.

The idea that this place was our secret, though, had been damaged. Evidence of another vehicle driving beyond the suburbs to our four-lane broke our belief that only we knew this road. A belief in singularity, in possession, is the protection of youth. Growing up was the realization that someone has been here before and that all roads have somewhere to go.

To get to the four-lane you have to turn off 94th South, toward Draper where all the horse properties were being turned into small castles and pretend-lodges—each house a one-time forest of its own now siding, now balcony—some with redwood, some cedar—all wood, all imported to this alpine-desert city where scrub oak and junipers and a few Doug-firs made up the green specks in the otherwise mostly ochre landscape. Follow along Dimple Dell road—the same one my grandpa used to take us to see the horses when we were younger—turn left, and then take a right on the road that curves back toward the mountains, into the foothills. And then that

curve stops. You're at the end of the road. You have to cross the dirt
road to move toward something entirely different.

The VW Fastback always took the ending of the pavement hard—
the all-metal dashboard clicked and clanged for the two hundred feet
or so until we were back on new asphalt, freshly paved, and onto the
unnamed, four-lanes going nowhere. This road started somewhere
suburban and dead-ended up here—in the foothills, flanked by
scrub-oak, at the edge of a flattened snake. Metal and rubber trump
dirt and scale.

~ ~ ~

Utah has seen substantial oil and gas exploration since
natural gas was first discovered in 1891. Oil and gas
production took off in earnest during the mid 1940s [1].
Since production first started, over 13,500 wells have been
drilled, covering much of the state, as shown in *Figure 1*.
Total oil production as of October 2003 has been 1.24
billion barrels (BBO); total gas production has been 7.65
trillion cubic feet (TCF). The United States presently uses
approximately 19.6 million barrels of oil (MMBO) a day and
62 billion cubic feet (BCF) of natural gas a day [2]. Thus, over
the past 65 years, enough resources have been produced to
supply the U.S. with oil for just over two months and gas for
about four months at today's rate of consumption.

http://action.suwa.org/site/PageServer?pagename=
library_LemkinReport

My dad drove a VW Karmann Ghia when he was in college. In my mind
the car was painted purple, the shade I swore he told me he dyed his
hair. But purple hair would have been far too wild even for his hun-
dred-mile-an-hour-driving ways and I don't think they, even these
days, paint cars purple. When I was thirteen, my dad drove a Cadillac
even though his mother's side of the family has always been committed
to the Buick. In the most suburban of ways, my dad was still rebelling.

My twin sisters, Paige and Val, and our mom and dad are sitting
around the kitchen table for dinner like we do most nights. We are

eating stir-fry. My mom, when she cooks with water chestnuts and thin strips of steak and soy sauce, is a more adventurous cook than most of my friends' moms. She also recycles.

My dad is trying to convince us that it would be a good idea to take a new job and to move to Houston. We, my twin sisters and I, do not want to go. We'd lose our friends. Our school. Our house with its many good-for-hiding closets.

"It's hot there, Dad," we respond. "It's humid," we complain. "I've heard there are snakes all over there," I argue. I picture a back-yard, green like our over-watered lawn here but, if you look closely, it moves, undulates. The Houston backyard is a seething mass of green-backed snakes and soft lawns. My dad tells us that he would be the president of a company—no longer the vice-president of re-search, not the VP of sales, but the president. He would tell the buy-ers what kind of drill bits to look for. He would decide whether or not to pursue extracting oil from shale rock. He would decide if it was wise to wring crude from beneath the twisted Colorado River.

I give him a stone-cold look and tell him that there is no way that I am going to Houston, Texas, to live with all the green and rain and snakes.

He tells me I'll go where he tells me to go.

But we don't end up moving to Houston even though the oil in-dustry was booming for the first time since my dad had become a geological engineer. The job would have let him be a star—president of his own drilling research lab. He'd be home more, travel less to Venezuela and France. He could get out from under the shadow of Christensen Diamond, his family's diamond-drill bit business where my dad's job was as much thanks to nepotism as his cousin's even though my dad had a master's in geology from Columbia and his cousin barely had his high school diploma.

Instead of moving to Houston, he continued to go to work every day with a sandwich, topped with unusual condiments like horse-radish and red bell peppers, that my mom made him. His office had chalkboards on three walls. He'd work some math problems in the morning detailing some exercise in force and mass and pounds per square inch. He'd walk down the hall for coffee. His great-uncle

Frank, the president of the company, would invite him in, pour some bourbon in my dad's mug and tell him to get on the phone with some clients, to bring him some buyers and stop wasting his time with all that chalk. That's for drilling. We sell diamonds, he told my dad. Ugly and big diamonds. The only science you need to know is that the bigger, the better.

~ ~ ~

Mark's hand was on my knee. No pressure. It was just a gesture. A friend of the Bishopric, his role, had been appointed to drive me home. I was just a Mormon girl, my role, with a shocking inability to call my parents for a ride. That's the kind of girl I could learn how to be. Don't we turn here? I asked with pretend innocence. Oh, let's take the back-way, Elder Mark suggested.

It wasn't enough that he was seventeen and I was fourteen and he was teaching me to drive—telling me about the power of first gear, reminding me to let go the pressure with my left while applying pressure with my right. It wasn't illicit enough for the bark of the scrub oak to rub against my naked back. I had to become the Mormon girl I never had been. The one who didn't occasionally smoke one of Mark's Camels, except now here, he's offering me one. Although Joseph Smith's Words of Wisdom prohibited some kinds of smoking, if you were a member of the priesthood, there are rules that can allow for all kinds of things. The priesthood—a cabal of men who know just what's good for you—play many roles: interpreter of God's will, emissary to the prophet, instructor of women, father to the children, especially the girl-children who need so much guidance.

Role-playing is a bit about pressure—the way you have to not giggle, have to stay in character, have to pretend you're wearing a modest dress rather than a pair of shorts that your boyfriend gave to you back when he was playing the role of your boyfriend instead of the role of your Bishop. The way the hand on your leg can't move too quickly to your thigh. The way the roles constrict and confine you so much that you almost can't move, and if you do, the hand grips your thigh a little more tightly. When he stops the Fastback by the ring of scrub oak, I pretend to ask him why I should get out although I know there's already a blanket laid out under the ring of trees. As the good girl I'm pretending to be, I obey my Bishop when he suggests I lie down, when he suggests that perhaps I should unbutton my shirt to cool down. The Bishop, you know, has already baptized me, laid my whole body down in the water. He's seen my body through the sheer white of my christening gown. Why not look at it through the gauzy filter of the too-bright sunlight. When he lies down upon me—all two hundred of his pretend Bishop-like pounds, hairy as a Bishop, tall as a Bishop, as practiced as a Bishop saying that the parting of the legs is like Moses parting the sea and if God didn't want it to happen, then the legs wouldn't part. Obviously, the Mormon girl and God are in cahoots. The legs and seas are parted for the Bishops and the Moseses of the world. I lie still and try to feel soft though I can feel my body hardening under the weight and the pressure and the metaphors begin to mix: how much disappearance is required for transformation? Where did the innocent Mormon girl I pretended to be go? She was just around here—her grandmother took her to Sunday school. She drank the sacrament from the little paper cups. She ate the cubed Wonder bread as it came down the aisle. Sometimes she took two pieces. Sometimes she thought she was more Mormon than her own mother or her own father who had been baptized in this religion, who had grown up thinking there was no substitute for the one right church. Of course, they didn't consider the nature of the church tended toward plurality with its polygamy and multi-tiered heaven. Perhaps Mormonism is the religion of metaphor, transference, and transformation. It is also the church of fathers who are Bishops, unpaid lay-priests who sometimes forget who are their daughters and who are their wives or have a unique capacity to let their women be both, simultaneously. I did not, in our role-playing, have to call Mark "Father." That is a Catholic honorific that denotes celibacy and marriage to the Church. In the Mormon faith, any man can hold the priesthood, hold the bishopric. In a sense, all the men are fathers, even if not your own, elementally.

We go to the four-lane because it's the end of the road. Because there are no other cars on this almost-highway. There will be, when the ground is dug out from the hillside and the snakes are baited and the scrub oak is torn from its roots and the developers build mini-lodges there under the shadow of the mountain. But for now we're here because there's a paved road—except for that one dirt bit that's nearly impassable for a 1967 Volkswagen, and the privacy provided by scrub oak.

~ ~ ~

Scrub oak grows in a circle. It surrounds you like a wreath or a maze. Its provenance is distinctly western although what it exactly is, is hard to discern. On the Internet there is little information. There's a disambiguated Wikipedia entry. There's a paper by Tom Chester who discovered that *Quercus berberidifolia,* the best-known species of scrub oak, is not as widespread throughout the west as he once thought. There are other kinds of scrub oak mixing in with *berberidifolia*—it's hard to pick out what's scrub and what's not.

But the genus name, the same as all oak, *quercus,* sounds like query, sounds like question, sounds like open, come in here and hide, come into my closet, and I'll take you to another world *The Lion, The Witch and The Wardrobe*-style, come into this species that is undefinable, unfindable, unwikipediable, and lie on the ground. Quercus sounds quirky and odd and isn't it better to be odd than normal, those short little stubbies, scrubbing the foothills with their bristle-brush leaf-heads. *Quercus berberidifolia, Quercus acutidens,* you are all things teenage—carpet and correct, flowers and Accutane. Your side effects are usually dermis-related—rashes and blotches, eczema and acne, but sometimes you open up, let in to feed the woodpecker. Let in a western snake—a rattler, a yellow-bellied racer, or, most likely, a rubber boa mound in the V between root and trunk. Take care, rubber boa. Four lanes are a lot of lane to cross. Even when traffic is light.

Quercus sounds like want. And like want, although it has many subspecies, its genus never changes.

Scrub oaks are not the kind of trees that become diamonds. You need a rainforest for that—the kind where the ground is so wet and the leaves are so thick they give off as much moisture as the clouds that rain down do. In the temperate rainforest in December, it's cold enough that the earth is sending up its water and you can't tell if it's raining from above or below. In December in the temperate rainforest, your shoes have drenched your socks and even your Gortex has begun to seep. You step from fallen tree to fallen tree until one decays into dirt right under your foot and you fall into a fern and your pants that were damp before are fully wet now thanks to the leaves shaking their spores and rain onto you. In the rainforest, all this water lets the trees grow fast. It lets the ground absorb the fallen trees. The mushrooms dig in and break up solid matter—cleaving a red cedar trunk with its hard conch shell or moving moss this way and a fern that with the fluted edges of a chanterelle. Things go up fast—or fast for tree time—and for a long time. All that tree sucking up all that carbon, pumping out the oxygen back into the sky. The carbon builds thick trunks and wide branches. It builds canopy and systems of roots. The carbon is pumped up by rain and then put down into the ground by more rain and mushroom, by time and the weight of a thousand pounds of water tucking it deep into the ground. Dig with your hand deep into the dust. You'll find the carbon remnants of a thousand old trees that fell a thousand years ago. Sit on it. Fell another tree upon it. Let broken branches and dusty lichen, fern spore and ash leaf crush. Bring down an ice age upon it. Bear upon it all the weight of your fathers and their fathers' fathers. Tamp it down like the moist tobacco in a pipe. Be patient. Let the tectonic plates shift. Let a mountain or two rise and begin to fall. Then begin to dig—first you'll need a machine to dig the diamond. Then take that diamond and dig deeper until all that water has turned into a buried sea of unreflecting memory. The forest relieved of pressure spews.

~ ~ ~

The drilling of oil is not as romantic as all that. Press the collar firmly into the cool desert sand. Tuck of metal digs into the ground like you would attach the parchment of a lamp shade to its metal cast—somehow the marrying of pliable surface to unbending alloy makes the coupling secure. Ease your drill bit and the pipe in the hole. Attach the kelly—the pipe that transfers rotary motion to the turntable wand to the turntable itself and begin drilling. Turn on the motors, powered by diesel engines. Don't forget to attach the bit—use a diamond if you have one. You're going through rock here. Through sludge and shale. This is the past you're digging through. You'll need to circulate mud through the pipe and out of the bit to float the rock cuttings out of the hole. There's a lot of stuff in there and no way for it to get out if you don't flush it out. Something's got to disappear before something new can appear. Add new joints as the sections get deeper. Yell something loud when you've found what you were looking for.

~ ~ ~

Sometimes Mark played the father-figure role: I was only fourteen but he was teaching me to drive on the four-lane. The fastback had a manual transmission. I was short and the seat's tracks, worn out from twenty years of slipping back and forth, were stuck back, so I had to scoot to the end of the seat to reach the pedals. We didn't worry about the cops. As soon as we crossed from the pavement of subdivision and onto the stretch of rock and bare dirt, we were moving into our own land with our own laws. The laws of drivers' ed, along with a few other laws, simply evaporated. If you discover a road that seemingly goes nowhere, doesn't it mean it's meant for you? Nowhere doesn't have many rules and there, you can pretend to be whomever you want to be.

Later, my dad officially taught me to drive. He gave me driving hints and cautionary tales from the time I was ten. "Always check your blind spot." "In the time it takes to sneeze, an oncoming car could slam into you." I never knew if I should take this to mean that I should not sneeze or not close my eyes when I sneeze or not drive during allergy season. I would nod my head rather than ask. He said it with such authority, like he was the president of a company or at least the driver with the best insurance rating, like the driver he had been before the DUIs, when he drove his Karman Ghia. Unlike when Mark was teaching me to drive, far out on the flat four-lane, my dad took me to the subdivision dug high-up into the foothills. But like Mark, he made me brake with my right, keep my left on the clutch, and then quickly move brake foot to accelerator foot, letting out the clutch so slowly that an ant might well have been pushing the car. I stalled the car a couple of times but I made it up the hill. My dad was impressed with my quick study and the fact that I never let the car roll backwards. Teaching was not a role my dad was particularly good at. He lost his patience quickly, taking the hammer out of my hands when I pounded the nail crooked, erasing the math steps I'd scribbled down wrong, clipping the transistor into the right wires of the radio I was making. But since I already mostly knew how to drive, Dad was pleased with his good parenting.

The press and release I had learned from Mark but the timing, I learned from my dad. He let me drive all the way home meaning I had to cross four lanes of traffic, stop and start and make it up one more hill. I wanted to be a good driver like my dad. I kept my hands at ten and two. I tried not to sneeze.

~ ~ ~

Gasoline engines work a lot like a sneeze. Well, not really so much, but a little. A sneeze is, according to the Benadryl spokesperson Patti Wood, a sudden, violent, spasmodic, audible expiration of breath through the nose and mouth. A sneeze is irritant plus lung power, plus spit. An engine, at the cause and effect level, converts, via gasoline and spark plug, carbon into motion. The pistons act like lungs pushing the oxygen outward.

1. $C + O_2 = CO_2$
2. $H + O_2 = H_2O$

There are tiny bombs going off in your car. The reason for the anti-knocking devices in modern gasoline is to reduce the percussive explosions created by the mad mixture of gas, air, and fire. The spark plug fires. The gas responds appropriately. Additional chemicals and the fine art of modern-day computer-monitored fuel injectors that keep the amount of oxygen just so to prevent the cracking of the engine block, the loosening of the bolts and gaskets, or, in worst case scenarios, the entire blowing up of the car. It's a tricky balance, packing the past into the small interior of your tank and using the smallest amount of immediate fire to propel your automobile ever so slightly into the future.

~ ~ ~

Mark smoked Camels. My dad smoked Benson & Hedges. Each brand tells something about what each man thought he wanted to be. The same tobacco, for the most part, goes in between the paper although the Benson & Hedges filter matches white unlike the flecked-gold paper of the Camel. B & Hs are also thinner and therefore, more refined, or perhaps effete, looking. Cowboy versus sophisticate is how those signs read supposedly differently. And yet it is still dried leaf and dry paper burning into so much nothing. If it wasn't for the smoke and the butt, you'd never know that sign existed at all. If Mark and Dad had exchanged cigarette brands, would Mark have started wearing cufflinks and learning French via book tape on the drive to work? Would Dad have started riding a moped and wearing jeans ripped wide with holes?

Carbon plus oxygen turns cigarettes to smoke, gasoline to air, men into metaphors. A sea of cars during rush hour is propelled by pressed plankton never seen by human eyes. Only the polar bears seem to notice the heat from tailpipes rising along with the sky-bound plants.

It's hard to see my dad at all through the haze of smoke and memory. When I google Bruce H. Walker, the searches return only a link for an ophthalmologist and one for a hotel management company. Nothing about a geologist who smoked Benson & Hedges, who knew a lot about diamonds, who had introduced his kids to the Internet as early as 1985. As far as the Internet is concerned, my dad has completely disappeared. Sometimes though, the sight of a single, narrow cigarette brings the history, if not the man himself, back.

~ ~ ~

Mark and I spent most of our time together driving around in the Fastback. Leaded gas was eighty-five cents a gallon and, while the black stuff that puffed out the muffler didn't seem particularly healthy, no one had even suggested that the invisible stuff we were pumping out the back of the exhaust pipe was layering itself against the atmosphere, glazing the sky in sheets of glass that could build so thick and reflect back only so much light and grow so heavy, that all that glass might shatter, raining in hot sluices all that pressed forest back down upon our heads. The heat that was in the ground was converted in the car. Laws of conversion should have warned us but we were convinced only by what we could see. The gas smelled so much like old fire going in and like nothing when it came out. We had no need to think of it again.

So we drove, down by the Old Mill where the Big Cottonwood River drained and the mill's walls and fences made of river stones were collapsing back into the river, we drove downtown and turned the car toward our suburb way out south and watched the lights warm the valley, we drove by the four-way and we drove down 7th East—the six-lane road that connected the suburb to the downtown and where I imagine I have spent the bulk of my driving-life. It was on the freeway exit onto 7th East where the policeman pulled us over. Mark's car had expired plates. So expired that they made us get out of the car. That they put us in the back of the police car. That I sat on the blue vinyl seats and looked at the place where locks should have been but where none were, and waited while they called Mark's mom. Mark's dad showed up unexpectedly with Mark's mom in his boat of a Ford Galaxy. We squished into the back with his brothers. Mark's dad, who drank as much as my dad but came home far less often and punched holes in walls a lot more often, went off alternately about being responsible enough to get the emissions fixed so his damn car would register and about being lucky to not be hauled off to jail for driving a fourteen-year-old girl around.

Who was this guy pretending to be a father, blown in on the wind, acting like authoritarian, know-it-all father as he drove the boat of a car down the road?

I pretended I wasn't there. Mark pretended I wasn't there. His mom gave me a short smile and I turned to look at Mark's car as the tow-truck's hook dug under the front panel. I watched as the truck towed the car down 7th East and made a left on 21st and drove out of sight, disappearing like all the first elements do.

The Fastback, like the Karmann Ghia, turned into a more practical car that took unleaded gas and had functioning seatbelts. I haven't seen Mark in longer than I haven't seen my dad. The Fastback, like the Karmann Ghia, unlike the four-lane, turned into nothing. Smoke.

The four-lane, now a mini-highway, is full of traffic, lined by stop signs and mini-mansions, completely devoid of snake and oak.

10,000 Deserted Lakes

Minnesota is the land of ten thousand lakes. It is also the land of ten thousand rehab facilities. At least it seems like that many. My dad had been to others. He went to in-town rehabs. At Charter Canyon in Salt Lake, he learned the fall back into a stranger's arms routine. He memorized the lines to make amends. He learned that one drink, you're off the wagon. Which is how he learned that once you're off the wagon, you may as well stay off and walk. At least when you're walking, you can hold your booze with one hand and into the wall with the other. At Betty Ford, he learned how to rap with one of the Ices and he learned that he didn't make nearly as much money as he needed to if he was going to spend two months a year rehabilitating and ten months of the year disabilitating.

It was a last ditch effort, this place in Minnesota. It was a new program, he told me and my sisters. A new kind of rehab. The kind where you need neither God nor chips to hang on your key-ring. This kind of rehab teaches cognitive behavior therapy, he told us. For ten thousand dollars, he wouldn't need Antabuse. He wouldn't need twelve steps. All he would need is to re-learn how to drink. How one was enough. How wagons were meant for social drinkers and occasional tipplers. He told us that's what he wanted. To go to an Oktoberfest and have one beer. To go to a wine-tasting. To accept the offer of a sip of forty-year-old scotch and stop at the sip. It's a reasonable request. Ten thousand dollars for a new brain didn't seem like all that much. We told him to go. He made the phone calls. He never bought the ticket.

10,000 Liters

The average Western family uses ten thousand liters of water a month. Almost four thousand gallons. That's counting only the household—drinking and flushing, washing dishes and cars and clothes and kids. That doesn't even count the water used to grow the cow to make the steak we'll grill for dinner or the water we used to water the potatoes we'll bake or roast or fry. It takes one thousand liters of water to produce one kilogram of potatoes. To produce a kilogram of beef, you'd need forty-two thousand, three hundred liters—ten thousand gallons. Think of how very thirsty French fries make you and how quenched a bite of steak does. Think how much wet heat you need to boil potatoes; think how dry the charcoal is. Cows are thirsty creatures. If you count the streams they trample and divert from contributing to larger channels, cows suck up or tread down almost twenty thousand gallons of water per kilo of beef. If that's kilo per whole cow or kilo per butchered carcass, I'm not sure. It is said that one can live on only thirty liters a day, nine-hundred liters a month, to subsist. Five a day for eating and drinking and twenty-five for hygiene (as thirsty as cows are, we are as dirty). Where does the other nine thousand, one hundred liters go? Eighty-gallon capacity bathtubs, hosed-down sidewalks, half-full dishwashers and the Kleenex that had to be flushed. And more for the steak. And the potatoes.

Minnesota

Utah has plenty of lakes. Small ones and big ones and salty ones. Ones made from dammed rivers and natural mountain lakes so clear the shale that lines the bottom thirty feet below shines green enough it seems you could touch it. Utah has plenty of lakes but they're far apart, cold, shallow, mountainous, prone to dry up in August when you really need them or full of motor boats when you want to swim.

Minnesota is a kind of lake-territory I never knew. Different than Oregon too, for Oregon's lakes are mountainous like Utah's. Rivers dominate Oregon's geography. And although many big rivers begin in Minnesota lakes define it, industrially, aesthetically, recreationally—they are populated. Lakes are for fishing, for living around, for camping by, for swimming, for floating. These are human-integrated lakes. Recreational lakes. Warm enough to dive into in the summer and cold enough to skate across in the winter. In the summer, the banks are lined with fishermen and from boats of every size, raft to yacht, reels hang. In the winter, fishermen slide little huts out over the frozen lake. Cut circles into ice and toss their fishing line into the water.

The best recipe for lake trout: Gut and remove all the viscera. Place a stick through the cavity of the opening you made while gutting the fish. Push the stick all the way through the fish's head. Place rocks on the sides of hot coals from the campfire. Let the stick rest over the coals. The fish can now hang over the fire. Watch the fish closely. If the tail sets on fire, put it out. When the fish has turned from the pink when you first sliced it open to gray-white, the fish is cooked. Remove the stick from the fish. Add salt and pepper. Add a tablespoon of butter. Just one. There is only so much butter and we still need to cook breakfast tomorrow. Conserve the heat of the fire. Stoke the coals. Fan up the flames. You don't know how cold it gets at night with the breeze off the water.

Hard Water

Las Vegas was once a small settlement named Bringhurst, but it got its current name from the grasslands (*las vegas*, the meadows) that once grew in the valley. In the desert, grass represents a shallow water table, and in the Las Vegas Valley grass was a sign of the natural faults that force the water table near the ground surface there.

Las Vegas languished as a tiny railroad town, serving the nearby mines, until the Colorado River was dammed to create Lake Mead in the 1930s. The city has also exploited the aquifers beneath the Las Vegas Valley so that even if the city vanished tomorrow, the meadows would not return. The availability of enough water to boat in and fill pools helped turn Las Vegas into the tourist destination it is today.

> *http://geology.about.com/od/geology_*
> *nv/a/lasvegasgeology.htm*

Las Vegas's First Water

Las Vegas's first celestial purpose was to provide a stopover for Mormon Saints heading from Salt Lake to California. Its terrestrial purpose was to provide a drop of water at the edge of the Mohave Desert. Las Vegas, translated from the Spanish, means "The Meadows." Meadows because water was there. Meadows because there was a small tuft of green in a surrounding desert of tans and reds. Meadows meant refuge. A small band of Indians had lived there for awhile. Eventually though, everyone abandoned it: first the Indians, then the Mormons, then the railroad. Were it not for three godsends: the legalization of gambling, no-questions-asked divorces, and the building of the Hoover Dam, Las Vegas the place would be nothing but a vision.

The ground under Las Vegas is changing all the time. Vegas the city is changing all the time. I visited my cousin a lot when I was younger. I don't think I'd recognize it as the same place anymore. Now, I drive the long way around to avoid the place.

Vacation Las Vegas

Even though my cousin Michelle is woefully unaware of PIL, Johnny Rotten or the Sex Pistols, when I am twelve, I go to visit her over summer break. She has lived in Las Vegas since she and I were five and her mom followed her second husband to live down there in their under-furnished house, miles from the strip. It's stupidly hot to go down there in the middle of July, but since everyone has a pool and everywhere we go has air-conditioning, I return for my annual trip. And Aunt Bev will take us to Circus Circus and buy us caramel popcorn and let us ride on the rides. Even though I say I'm too old to like that stuff, the trapeze act still amazes me. I hold my breath when they let go. I close my eyes while they fall. I never manage to open them before the man has caught the woman. I open my eyes only in time to see their swing slowing down.

But when Aunt Bev's at work, we're more our pre-teen selves. Michelle knows some guys that we should invite over to come swimming. Brian, a boy from Michelle's class, lives two streets over. We don't know his phone number—only where he lives. We have to brave the heat, leave the air-conditioning. We think we'll be cooler running barefoot. We are wrong. The concrete is so hot that we have to run all the way there. By the time we get to his house, our feet are red with scrape and fire. We hop one foot to the other on the cement porch as Brian's mom answers the door. When she goes to get him from inside the refrigerated house, we try to cool our feet on the lawn. The grass cools but the individual blades, made defensive by unfaithful sprinklers and a lack of shade, prick the skin. We need to get into the water. But Brian, or Brian's mother, was making us wait.

Brian and his friend Justin appear at the door. We had been un-self-conscious in our bikinis until they arrive. But the moment they step out, they shaded by awnings, we under the broadcast light, I cross my arms in front of my chest. This isn't my territory and I feel doubly exposed.

"Hey," they say in unison and I realize we will have to do all the invitational work.

But it won't be too hard. Brian is the only boy in the city who doesn't have a swimming pool. How he convinces Justin to come over to his house without one on what must have been a hundred and six degree day, I don't know.

"You guys want to go swimming?" I ask. Michelle should be the one to talk since she knows them but this is the kind of fight we get into and rather than play out the "no, you do it" argument, I just go ahead and ask.

They don't answer immediately. I'm beginning to get that we're being a little bit dumb about this. Why didn't we look up their phone number? Why did we wear our bikinis out down the street? I real-ize my immodesty is not always as effective as I want it to be, that I'm not entirely in control of it. I play it up at home. I get undressed with the blinds open to let Tony Hall see in if he wants. Sometimes he flashes his bedroom light at me. His house is directly behind ours but separated by a huge, open lot where they will eventually build an LDS stake house. But for now, there's nothing between him, our strange semaphore and my belief that Tony Hall will like me more if I take my bra off when he can see. Which he can't. Our windows are an eighth of a mile away. But still, when my mom catches me, she pulls the curtains shut so fast they almost rip. To her, I am just

raw sex oozing out of my body, sliming everyone up. I know that
I've already crossed from good girl to bad, from tight to loose, from
control to wild, but to discover that my cousin, who is my age, who
leads us on the half-naked journey to beg of boys, is, in any way, as
indelicate, as out of control, as oozing as me, well, then, maybe my
badness is not so complete.

So instead of asking them again or hinting or winking or coyly
letting my bikini strap fall to my shoulder, I walk away.

I don't care about these boys. I don't live here. They don't go to
my school. They're certainly not Tony Hall who, at fifteen, drives a
scooter and kissed me once against the garage of the neighbors and
who, when he had the chance, didn't go further than the kiss.

Michelle follows, reluctantly. She has to go to school with these
boys. These are the A list boys. If she cares, she should do something.

She follows me.

The boys, because I don't care if they do, follow.

By the time we make it to the road we need to cross to get to
the pool, the boys have caught up. Our feet barely made it across
the first time and now that the street has bubbled in the hot sun for
seven minutes longer than the last time we passed, the tar is start-
ing to melt.

The boys are wearing shoes. Now we are jealous and in want of
what they have.

"Hop on," Justin tells Michelle. He crouches down and she
climbs on his back. Brian, though, not to be outdone, just swings
me up into his arms. They run us across the street, drop us down
and follow us, a few steps behind, to Michelle's pool. The guys' shorts
double as swim suits. They have their shirts off and are in the pool
before we are.

One clear sign that I'm much naughtier than Michelle: I notice
Brian's hard-on. I swim on my back in front of him until he swims
under me, tugs at the tie to my top. It doesn't come off. I swim
away. Brian follows me to the shallow end. I look over to see what
Michelle and Justin are doing. They're throwing rings into the pool
and swimming down to catch them. It takes them thirty seconds to

retrieve three rings each. By the time they throw them again and can't see us, Brian has pressed me against the wall and I'm kissing him. The chlorine on his tongue, the water evaporating on his lips, our hot foreheads pressing and our cool hands digging between wet nylon and sticky flesh. When Justin and Michelle surface, we pretend to splash each other. When they go under again, Brian takes a chance to lick my neck. For a twelve-year-old boy, he seems to know what he's doing.

Maybe this is how Brian survives a pool-less summer in Vegas.

Desert Desert Everywhere

In March of 2006, Las Vegas implemented stage II water restrictions. Residents can water outdoors only one day a week. Swimming pools and hot tubs may not be filled now if they're not already. Fountains can only spout if they re-circulate the water. The reservoirs are down to 64 percent capacity and as the summer sun pounds on, the water evaporates right off the surface of Lake Mead. There are no clouds nearby to return the evaporation as rain.

Strangely, the rules are in effect only in the spring. Accumulation of water must be more important than retention.

In the summer, the signs read 'swim away.' It's not a sign to tell you to leave town. Rather, it's an invitation to stay and swim. In fact, the Las Vegas Water District argues that, "Public and private swimming pools are not currently subject to drought restrictions. When pool water is managed efficiently, swimming pools actually use less water than grass covering the same area."

The District goes on to blame the Rocky Mountains for the lack of water. The lack of snow-pack north means less water for swimming so far south. The snow has tried to catch up but every year, the snow layers it on just a bit more thinly, starts to fly a little later and melts faster and earlier. Lately, there had been only one good year, where the snow felt like I remembered it—deep, lasting, truly wintery. Apparently though, no one told Vegas the drought was over. The snow melted but never made it all the way to the sweet blue pools of Nevada. Where did it go? Did we northerners drink it all? Suck it down by watering our lawns any old day of the week we wanted? Did we start filling our own swimming pools because, though it's not yet as warm as Las Vegas, thank God, Salt Lake City is 100 degrees in May and a little dip might be just the thing? Move north, I remind myself. Keep moving north.

Establishing Boundaries

I wanted to be more like rock than water. I didn't want to be so easily moved from one side of the swimming pool to the other. I didn't want to be like the Colorado, pooling up against a man-made border. I wanted my own borders. I wanted to be the shifting tectonic shelf, but I didn't know how to do that. It was so much easier to let boys swirl their fingers through my hair, to splash against my buckling skin, to feel like they were falling deeply into me. But, just like a lake that permits a rudder's plunge, once the boat is docked, the water slides back over. I wanted change. I also wanted to shore up my own self.

This did not happen. Maybe because I'm a Scorpio and a water sign, I'm destined for some gentle pushing around, not hard, forward moves.

I did keep moving. I tried to go north and toward water. I moved away to college even though David, the boyfriend I almost couldn't leave behind for a three week vacation, couldn't come with me. He tried to move to Portland with me but the $80 he'd brought with him to rent an apartment near campus was not enough. He returned to Salt Lake and I stayed in Portland where everything is lush and water isn't just something to be pushed around. In Oregon, water makes its own path—it forces the landscape as stubbornly as rock. I was making choices. Well-reasoned ones although if I had known that David couldn't come with me before I got there, would I have gone? I still shifted in the stream of boys' opinions.

WATER, WATER EVERYWHERE

The journals of the Lewis and Clark expedition contain the
oldest meteorological records for Oregon. When the explorers
camped here in the winter of 1806, their diaries contained
numerous brief entries that are nearly identical: "hard rain
all last night, and continues as usual." Or, "It rained hard all
last night, & still continued the same this morning." And, "It
continued Raining during the whole of this day."

> *http://www.opb.org/programs/oregonstory/water/*
> *or_water/page_1.html*

The Mormons Move at the Behest of a Higher Opinion

The Mormons were run out of Nauvoo, Illinois. They followed the
Oregon Trail for the first half, smartly trekking along rivers—the
North Platte, the Platte, the Missouri. They set up winter camps
at lush places, waited out the rain and the subsequent mud that
threatened to sink, then stop them. Participants in communal living meant that they needed to bring only one spinning wheel, one
piano—the stuff of community. The stuff of self-sufficiency.

So why, instead of following the Oregon Trail to the ever-lush
Willamette Valley, did they take a sharp left and follow the ill-fated
path of the Donner Party? The place they turned, the corner of
Wyoming, it seems, was the place where real need for basic sustenance should supplant the imagined need that God wants you to go
to make a garden of the desert and establish a new world. At least
it would to me. Taking a left means giving up big rivers and heavy
rains for tiny rivers and big snow. But they believed in something
more than the land of plenty. They believed in making plenty out of
nothing. They chose hardship and difficult soil on purpose.

In the end, they've met their God's agenda and, in the last century and a half, successfully fulfilled most basic needs. Irrigation
may be a hallmark of the west but it also confirms that Brigham was

right: you can make a garden out of desert by migration—migrate yourselves, your spinning wheel, your fine china and your chicken and you will be strong enough, or smart enough, or blessed enough to migrate the snows out of the mountains and across the acres of the valley. You can hear the spirit of move through every water pipe.

Generational Vegas

When he was eighteen, Mike Press and my dad drove from Salt Lake City to Las Vegas, about four hundred miles, in five hours. What did they do there that everyone doesn't do? Drink too much, feel up too-naked girls, spend too much money, get stuck by the craps table because you just saw a seven roll by and in fourteen minutes or less it's going to be your turn. That's what eighteen-year-olds do, even twenty-five-year-olds. But, at some point, you're expected to be able to rein in those appetites. One should be able to get a handle on his compulsions and, for once, say, I think this fifth shot will be my last. One should be able to, after walking out of the first titty bar, go home and masturbate, not exchange another twenty for ones and go where the girls are seedier and the poles slipperier. One should be able to, when the 7's have lined up only once when you put one quarter in and should have put in all three for that thousand dollar pay-off, you should be able to stand up, walk outside, take a breath of fresh air. But no one goes to Vegas for the air. They go there for the too much, and my dad went there too often.

Water Therapy

In college, I saw a counselor once, after my boyfriend and I broke up. She told me to try to go on a real date with a guy before I slept with him or invited him to move in. I did not know exactly what she meant.

"It's not about not having sex. Have all the sex you want. It's about time. Slow down."

I wasn't sure what a date looked like but I did start taking Chris to lunch at Nordstrom's café. I was paying but we weren't sleeping together. That seemed like a good start.

The Draw

The meadows originally attracted travelers stopping by what was originally called Big and Little Springs for a picnic lunch, deer coming out of the canyon to drink, grasses finding a place to green themselves. No one stops by this old watering hole any more. The watering hole they find is the spectacular Bellagio Fountain or maybe the Bellagio's bar. But there are plans to make this once-upon-a-time place into a nature preserve or, perhaps more accurately, a natural history museum, since no water makes it to the surface anymore.

The springs dried up in the 1960s but full-scale reconstruction has begun. There's a pueblo dwelling, an array of plants. Birds have been imported. They plan to have trails and theatrical performances and possibly weddings. The original spring that may have lured you to stopover for a swim or a drink may be gone, but they're putting in a pool. The ground is easy to dig. Pliable, malleable, ready for whatever man-made lining you can bring her. Concrete rolls in on trucks. Snow melts in the northern mountains. Pipes are laid. The water pressure against the Hoover Dam builds. Eventually, water pushes back, even if it's against man-made constructs and rigid shells.

Dam

(dame, lady, female parent, barrier checking the downward
flow of water, bridge)

I missed my mom when I was at college. I couldn't tell her that. Doing so would not testify to my seventeen-year-old grown up self. I did, however, spend a lot of time driving back and forth across Portland's bridges, listening to her favorite music—Janis Ian, Simon and Garfunkel. There was a song she used to sing me before bed when I was very little that I'd look for every time I went to Tower Records. Take this hammer, were the lyrics. I could never find the song and I was too shy to ask. Even if I had, who would have directed me to Johnny Cash or folk musicians? The guys who worked at Tower knew Public Enemy, Firehose, not mom-songs.

Since I couldn't find the song, I wrote my own lyrics that went something like, ain't no hammer on this mountain, shines like mine, shines like mine and the only thing that it smashes is the dam with you behind. Take this hammer, take it to the captain, with these handprints that are mine, for breaking walls and building bridges, the only thing you got is time.

I never gave my mom the song but I did eventually find Johnny Cash singing his version of the John Henry song and I still think of my mom whenever I hear it, even though the real song has nothing to do with the good things about bridges.

In college, I learned to despise a dam. What they did to the fish could not be undone. And I still cry when I cross the Glen Canyon Dam bridge. But some of those early, smaller dams—they held things back. They hold things back—sometimes for the good, sometimes for the bad. They protect from floods. They change the landscape.

They make a boundary, false though it may be, between up-lake and down-river.

My mother does this:

She bites her pinkie finger when she's upset to make herself not cry.

She drinks chardonnay.

She always says what she means even if that means telling my friend Pete that she doesn't like the red pants he's wearing or my friend Jeff that all writers had tortured lives and if they didn't they can't be real writers or telling the waiter that the music is too f-ing loud.

She actually says "f-ing."

She doesn't swear except to say god or damn or Jesus. Usually in the same phrase.

She expresses her disgust by throwing her head to the left and pushing a "th" sound out from between her teeth.

Sometimes eye-rolling accompanies the sound.

Sometimes her head turns away completely. If her shoulders get involved in a sort of humping shrug, you know you've committed a seriously egregious faux pas, like saying it's OK to put a shoe with gum stuck on it in the freezer to freeze the gum off. Something like that may even make her shoulder twitch.

She knows how to say no.

The main lesson at the dinner table was restraint. Singing was prohibited. As were elbows on the table. You must cut your salad greens into manageable bites. Eating too quickly or talking with food in your mouth—not allowed. Nor was salting your food before tasting it. Dad would always tell the cautionary tale of the guy who was interviewing for a job at IBM. The interview continued into lunch. The guy salted his food before he tasted it. He did not get the job. My dad took from it that the guy was presumptuous and to succeed at IBM, you should test all hypotheses before jumping to conclusions about blandness. Dad never mentioned whether ordering a glass of wine before the other guys could have cost him the job as well.

After we were done eating, my sisters and I had to ask to be excused and take our plates to the dishwasher. All good lessons, in the end, I think. We ended up to be relatively well-mannered people, if overly-conscious of how we appeared to others and nervous about salt. My dad, though, had a problem with mustard. Maybe he had a problem with condiments in general, but in particular, whenever he'd get mustard on the side of his mouth, my mother's shoulder would twitch and eyes would roll. Jesus, she'd swear, and reach over to rub the offensive yellow off his face, like she was scraping gum off a shoe.

It was one of the few things she felt she had over him. He made the money, was supposedly the "smart" one, did the taxes, drafted blueprints for the hot tub room. But she out-classed him with a re-fined etiquette and a distaste for mustard, especially on one's face in the corner of one's mouth.

The building of the Glen Canyon Dam began in 1956, the year my mother turned 10. By the time I was born, twenty-five years later, it was finished and finally nearing capacity—3700 feet above sea level. The Glen Canyon Dam website quietly notes that, "The controversy surrounding the construction of the dam is often cited as the beginning of the modern-day environmental movement."

Cited reasons for said environmental movement:

Changes: Glen Canyon Dam has created a new Colorado River. Before the dam was built, water temperatures in the river fluctuated seasonally from 80°F (26°C) in the summer to near freezing in the winter. Now, the water temperature below the dam averages 46°F (7°C) year-round. The Colorado River was once filled with silt and sediment. Now, the river deposits its load of silt as it enters Lake Powell near Hite, Utah. Water released from the dam is clear and the Colorado River is muddy only when downstream tributaries contribute sediment.

As the habitat has changed, so have plant and animal species. Native fish, unable to survive in the colder water, have left the river. Five species are now endangered. But this new habitat now supports a healthy trout population. Before Glen Canyon Dam, spring run-offs built and rebuilt beaches and sandbars and scoured away riverside vegetation. Now, sediment is trapped in Lake Powell and the dam prevents high river flows. Riparian vegetation now grows along river banks, creating habitat for mammals, birds, amphibians, insects, and reptiles.

http://www.nps.gov/glca/naturescience/hydrologicactivity.htm

Who wouldn't argue for these changes? Green grasses? Riparian riverbanks? Five species of trout to fish for instead of the near-extinct chub? Who wants to eat a fish called Chub, Sucker or Squawfish anyway? Whoever heard of Chub Amandine? These changes confirm what we value—constancy (in water temperature), greenery (in idylls), an end to flooding (predictability), and clear, see-through water (cleanliness). Glen Canyon Dam made a little slice of heaven beneath it. The dirty Colorado has been reformed. Once, the Colorado River menaced seven states and Mexico with its unreliable, unproductive silty water.

However, the effects aren't entirely ideal. The silt that used to be distributed throughout those seven states and Mexico is now backing up against the dam. The turbines move more slowly every year. The river used to empty into the Gulf of California. Now it serves those seven states and Mexico with potable water and some electricity, but reaches its delta in a mere trickle. As the river ends further and further from the shore, you'll be able to hear the clanging of empty pots as the seven states, plus Mexico, clamor for water.

When I was eight and my twin sisters five, our family and another family, the McDonalds, rented a houseboat on Lake Powell, the lake that Glen Canyon Dam makes. We five kids were already in our life-jackets, waiting for the Eagle One—the houseboat that would take us to Rainbow Bridge, to the Anasazi ruins up Moki Canyon. Our boat's wake would lap against two thousand miles of red-beach shoreline. Blue against orange are savage colors together. The Eagle One that we had reserved was a deluxe houseboat—two stories, two

bathrooms, and a waterslide attached to the back. Unfortunately, by
the time we got down to pick it up, the Eagle One was sinking toward the bottom of the lake.

Sandy and my mom took me and Lee on a dingy to investigate.
A corner of the Eagle One still angled out of the water—you could
tell by the smoothness of the paint and the purpose with which it
seemed to sink that this had been the nicest boat in all of Bullfrog
Marina. Sandy McDonald wanted to get a closer look. He asked
my mom to steer the dingy. She'd never driven a boat before—she
pulled too hard to the left and the boat went in fast circles around
the Eagle One. Sandy took over controls.

We had to drive 95 miles south to Wahweap, the marina near
Page, Arizona, to pick up the only houseboat left in all of Lake Powell. This houseboat was not so deluxe. It was a blue, barge-like thing
with a camper kitchen and only one bathroom with beds that pulled
out over the kitchen table, over the pilot's seat, over the lavatory.
In fact, the whole thing smelled like one big floating toilet to me.
Every time I flushed, I would turn to look down the drain and see
the blue lake opening up like a big eye. I felt bad for peeing on the
eye. I felt bad about everything that I imagined was at the bottom
of the lake—sunken houseboats and toilets and their attendant dis-
posables, batteries, and outboard motors. Even though the water is
more than five hundred feet deep in some places, I thought I could
hear the sound of metal on metal. I rushed out of the bathroom
to see if we had run across the sunken Eagle One, but it was just
my mom, standing at the smelly fridge, Lysol in hand. She was hitting the can on the side of the door to see if she could get more to
come out.

Everybody else was changing into their suits to go swimming.
Sandy stopped the boat as my dad watched from the deck, drink
in hand. We jumped into the sun-soaked lake. We floated in our
faded lifejackets, felt the air bubble up by our ears, evaporating, and
smelled the diesel of other boats wafting by.

Over the sounds of motors, I could hear my dad asking Sandy if
he could drive. I could hear my mother say if he wanted to drive the
boat, he shouldn't have drunk an entire bottle of wine before din-

ner. Sandy tried to explain that as a meteorologist, he had more experience steering boats. Dad was a good swimmer, Sandy explained. Maybe he should keep an eye on the kids. My dad emerged from the cabin to watch us play in the water, a new drink in his hand.

We never vacationed with another family after that.

Filling Lake Powell didn't only erase petro glyphs, wind impressions and water expressions, it erased the names of places too. Kane Creek. Hidden Passage. Dungeon Canyon. Last Chance Canyon. Tapestry Wall. Hite Ferry. The places may still exist under the murky water. What strikes me most about the photos I've seen before Glen Canyon was filled is how varied the landscape is. Some of the photos remind me of other National Parks like Zions or Bryce or Capitol Reef, with their narrow canyons and red turrets and wind-painted rock walls. Other pictures remind me more of what the Mississippi River must have looked like over 200 years ago when there were no levies or locks or flood-management plans. The Colorado River, wide and meandering, looks like it has the patience, if not necessarily the power, to carve the Grand Canyon.

Even if they take down the dam, which some people want, there would still be evidence left behind, a large bathtub ring and all the Eagle Ones that had ever sunk. Congress would never fund removing the dam completely, only letting the water sink to its deadpool level—below any of the outflow tunnels. And while many of the canyons underneath have changed, the promise is that desert vegetation, wildlife, and sediment deposits will restore the canyons to their original beauty. Some things fulfill their promises, like when water returns a canyon to its originally-scheduled permanence.

Growing up, we lived behind a mortuary, a cemetery, and a Mormon church. The prospect of death seemed to follow us throughout suburbia. Even the Mormon Church, which had been built on a lot that promised to be kept "Open Space," haunted my parents. To my dad it meant patriarchal oversight, judgment, and offended his rationalistic atheism. To my mom it meant patriarchal oversight, abuse, Republicans, and offended her cosmopolitan sensibilities. When a mother would show up with six kids in tow, the oldest looking to be seven or eight, she'd shake her head and whisper "birth control" under her breath.

But when we lived behind the cemetery, no one complained about the neighbors. They were quiet and accommodating. The cemetery was one of the modern kind where no headstones stuck up, so the lawn mowers could drive their Toros from the driver's seat without needing to edge or weed whack or turn the steering wheel until they reached the fence that ran behind our house or one of our neighbors'.

Right behind our house, a small reservoir collected mountain run-off, enough to keep the cemetery green all summer long. A tall, chain link fence surrounded the concrete-bottomed pond, making it look as sculpted and manmade as the flat headstones that surrounded it. But maybe it was a natural pool, reinforced, fed by a spring rather than a dammed up little stream. The street we lived on was named Silver Lake. Maybe the reservoir had once been a beautiful, shimmering, natural lake. As I learned later, there are pockets of natural ponds all over Salt Lake Valley. Some are filled with mountain run-off, but others seem to have gathered in their depression with rain and snowmelt and a rupture in the aquifer. The cemetery's reservoir must have been made of the last kind because the dirt I dug in the backyard to build castles and moats felt more like soil than sand, more drenched than desert. Maybe it's why they built the cemetery there. If they'd built houses that close to the reservoir, they might have sunk in the swamp-like ground.

Plus, a natural natatorium would explain the salamanders. I don't know how old I was when I discovered them or how I convinced my younger sisters to crawl down into the window wells to dig for them with me, but during the summer, I would spring up from out of the tin-lined trenches that kept land from house with a new salamander every day. As my mom canned peaches and pears, apricots and pickles all summer, I would charge out with an empty Mason jar and back in with one full of a brown-speckled amphibian. Mom would punch holes in the gold lid to let in air and warn me to get some grass and water so the salamander wouldn't starve or die of thirst. I'd take the salamander back outside and play Wizard of Oz with him. I'd put the captive salamander at the top of the path my dad had dug into the wall of dirt that separated our yard from the cemetery. And then I would follow that path, singing that direction-filled song in the only direction the path led. The salamander was the wizard because he would have disappeared by the time I made it to the end of the song. I swore I'd screwed the lid on tight, but then, Mom was the last one to have touched it.

If salamanders were collectible trophies, then frogs were hidden treasures. My dad and I would sit out on the back patio and he'd list constellations and we'd listen to the frogs croaking from inside the fence of the reservoir. The crickets chimed in with frogs and the stars kept their names for the duration of the melody. My dad tried to explain about triangulation and how we knew how far away certain stars were, but the stars seemed closer to me than the frogs did. I was eight years old and I had never seen a frog. I'd seen a star. I could draw a triangle.

I convinced my friend Kim, who lived three houses up the street, that if salamanders were so easy to catch, frogs couldn't be much harder. It was accessing them that was the difficult part. The frogs had smartly cordoned themselves off from Mason-jar bearing kids. But the fence was not perfect. In one section of the perimeter, the metal had been wrenched up, leaving a gap between the fence and the ground just big enough for nine-year-old girls to slide through. I handed Kim the jar and tucked down to slide in first. I got my head through no problem but my shoulder got stuck on the wires. I tried to slide forward. I really wanted a frog. I tried to slide back out. I pushed and pulled and cut my arm on one of the links but there was no going anywhere. The frogs had eluded me and I was here, stuck.

Kim went to get her dad. Her dad went to get my mom. Kim's dad lifted the fence while my mom dragged me out. Of all the stupid things, she kept saying. You could have drowned, she kept saying. I'm not sure how I could have drowned if I was caught up on that fence like a scarecrow. The worst that could have happened, besides getting caught and getting no frogs, was that I could have been stuck there like the one time the salamander hadn't escaped from the jar. I didn't show this one to my mom and the air holes I had made were mostly cosmetic. I'd left him in the sun in the jar for a few days and he'd turned all white and desiccated. His flaky skin made my own skin itch.

The cervix is an amazing body part. Unlike the heart's perpetual motion, it moves only occasionally. Yet like the heart, as part of the uterus, this is one of the most powerful muscles in the human (female) body. The cervix has the power to hold in a nine-pound baby and its attendant placenta and amniotic sac while at its weakest—the closer a pregnant woman gets to labor, the thinner the cervix becomes. Some inverse relation occurs that when the unpregnant body needs to let sperm in or menstrual fluid out, this strong muscle moves only millimeters to allow passage. But, when pregnant, with up to forty pounds per inch pressure resting against it, the cervix stays zipped tight like a corset.

During labor, once the water breaks, the cervix goes from a pair of tight, puckered lips to gaping mouth in a matter of hours. From the size of a gaping mouth to the span of a gopher hole, the cervix dilates in another hour. From there, a breach: the cervix expands, wide enough to fit a baby's head. Very few other parts of the anatomy change so fast, so violently, so productively as the cervix. The heart beats or it doesn't. The blood flows or not. Over a lot of time, skin sags, fat cells grow. But the cervix, handy elastic that it is, stretches wide enough to turn a body inside out. And then it turns back again into tight, little puckered lips. It is simultaneously a dam and a bridge.

It used to snow a lot more. We walked to school in a tunnel of snow-plowed snow. We could barely see over what the shovelers had stacked on between the sidewalk and the curb. It snowed so much that my mom picked me and the twins up from school instead of having us walk the mile home.

We drove interminably slowly through the twenty-mile-an-hour school zone. Kids were throwing snowballs at my best friend Jeff, whose mom had not come to get him. My mom started yelling at the snowball-throwing kids. The snowballs burst against the metal of the cars. They bounced hard and small off of Jeff's back as if they had rocks in them. My mom yelled "stop it" again. Of course, the kids couldn't hear her. The windows were rolled up against the twenty-degree cold. But they could hear her fine when she pulled over and got out of the car.

"What in the hell do you think you're doing? You could break a window. You could hurt that kid. Give him an aneurysm." The kids squinted at her, snowballs in hand. My mother walked over to the kids and rose up to her full height—which was five foot nine in heels. She stood in front of Jeff, blocking off the other kids.

"Go ahead, throw." Her eyes grew thin as she waited for the kids to unleash their snowballs against her.

The kids scowled at my mom, but unconvincingly. One of the kids turned to look at me, his eyes threatening, "the next day." I shrugged right at them.

"Throw." She dared them.

The kids ran away. She scuttled Jeff into our car. She didn't stop yelling. "I don't know who the hell those kids think they are. I'm going to drive you guys home every day while it snows. I'm calling their mothers. They throw one more goddamned snowball at anyone . . ."

She didn't finish the threat. I think Jeff was more scared of her than the kids with snowballs. As she drove off, I rolled my window down and glared at the running kids as we drove by. I wanted to yell "goddamn" at them like my mother had, but I didn't. I was sitting safely behind her. I could have, but I, lacking her constancy, wavered. She delivered Jeff safely home and then told me to roll my window up. It was damn cold out there.

Skin of the Earth

In the winter light, streaming in from the obscured glass window, my face looks as cracked as the desert floor. The skin reads that there was once water there but that those days are over. The skin, as does the dirt, yawns for what it has lost. I rub Lubriderm into the cracks to the side of my eyes, in the middle of my forehead. I wonder if Botox would resolve the gap, would somehow make my brow a flat scape that promised a smooth ride from one side to the other, tripping no one up on my age or my past or how much sunscreen I neglected to wear in the high-altitude desert. If my skin is a map of cliché, then the legend is neither mystery nor code. The map is as plain as the porcelain I wished my skin to be.

After my dad died, we had him cremated. My sisters were twenty-one. I lived in Portland. We were not able to get it together to have him cryogenically frozen as he once said he'd like to be. My uncle's wife, who had been taking care of my dad, had found his body curled on the floor at the top of the stairs to the basement. He had not fallen down the stairs like his mother had or a friend of mine did. He did not make it that far. It was like he sat down, then laid down, then curled up. He was more cat than man then anyway. The funeral was what you'd expect from twenty-year-olds—full of 70s music like the Eagles' "Desperado," though he preferred the Linda Ronstadt version, and Don McLean's "Vincent" because who dies young who is not an artist? My dad once made a clay sculpture of tackling football players. Perhaps we thought that counted as art.

I went to see him before the cremation. He was still curled on the gurney. He had a bruise the size of a fist knotted in the skin of his forehead. The only person I could imagine making it was my dad himself. If you push into the brain far enough, perhaps you can change it.

After what seemed like the many-decade funeral, we gathered my dad's ashes up in a cardboard box housed in a purse of velvet and took him to the wake we thought he deserved. We sent him up in the style to which he had become accustomed. Bourbon-based Bloody Marys and chardonnay on ice. I drank gin and tonics at the time—differentiating myself from him, from those who thought a wake was a proper send-up. After too many gin and tonics, too many sips of bourbon and chardonnay, my mother and her sister and I opened the box. The ashes aren't uniform. There was obvious bone. I wet my finger with my tongue and stuck it in the box. I put my finger back in my mouth. The ashes tasted like nothing. Just dried out in the tuck and crevice of my throat. A kiln-firing from the inside out. Pottery shards become classic organs.

The earth's crust is alive. You think when you cup your hand and scoop a handful of grains, all you're doing is looking at the past—some shell a reminder that a lake was once here, that this was just a rock, that this grain was snail shell, this one was a Brontosaurus bone. But it's not true. The earth's crust moves. Like memory, it runs into itself, shaping itself as fluidly as sea.

My cuticles are falling apart. Every nail hangs. You can see the edges of my nails that soft skin usually hides. If drying is revealing. If drying is a pulling back. If the veil is lifted and now I see the contours of things best hidden, what behooves me to pull back further, to bite the skin, to tear at the white, now red, edges? If the bowl of Salt Lake Valley is the contour of God's cupped hand, when Lake Bonneville receded, did the plump ridges in the hand stretch flat, did the fatty mounds become fault lines stretched across palm and joint? Does the hand always cup or does it bend and crush and flatten? Do those mounds of finger flesh protect or do they promise landslide? Some say that if you can't trust the mountains then who can you trust? Gravity is constant. Water slides downhill. To quench a thirst, even a valley's, is inevitable.

The echoes of Lake Bonneville's shoreline are known for their isostatic rebound. The rigid surface layers float on top of a denser subsurface. The desert is water. Lake Bonneville, though dried up, still undulates and waves.

It took us a long time to decide when and how to spread the ashes. At first, the box they came in with its velvet wrapping sat on my mantel in what we thought was traditional cremation-having fashion. But the velvet attracted fireplace soot and animal hair, and the outside began to look a lot like the inside. I moved the box to my closet where I thought it would be warm and comforting and also warm and forgettable. The box was moved, by me, I suppose, to sit in the basement. So sat a lot of his books, his record collection—the Beatles, Mannheim Steamroller, Best of Bread, Roberta Flack, Gordon Lightfoot—which he'd recorded onto cassette tapes to keep the records from scratching. Eventually, my sister Val and I took half of the ashes to Hawaii. We spread them out on a beach of Kona named what I can't remember. There may have been a poem read or a joke about how he could find his way back toward the continent by following the current if he needed to.

Later, both my sisters and I took the rest of the ashes to Guardsman's Pass which was the tricky, back way to Park City. My dad drove us in his Buick or sometimes the Jeep over the dirt roads and we'd descend on our favorite restaurant—*Scrooges,* which was decorated like Christmas every day of the year except for December 25th, when they decorated for Halloween.

On the side of one of the few hills where condos weren't emerging, the twins and I got out, sat in the dirt with the stems of cheatgrass poking our legs, crinkled some fallen leaves in our hands, turned them to pieces. Paige told the story about the time he needed Ski Patrol to toboggan him down the mountain because he had over-medicated, one way or the other. Val reminded us about her first wedding and how he walked her down the aisle, crooked. I remembered the time at the castle in Germany when he almost fell off his chair. And the story too of how he let me help him build the redwood deck and room for the hot tub. How he pitched me softballs. How he taught me to ride a bike. The twins know those last stories less well than I, because I had him more sober for longer. It took him quite awhile to prefer drinks to kids. Of course, the day I lost my virginity was the day he started drinking, it seemed to me. The revelation of my sexuality drove him to hide behind liquor. But maybe not. Maybe the changes did not correlate. Maybe like water and salt, the two just dissolved into each other.

The ashes spread, Paige and Val and I headed back to Salt Lake. Park City was a resort town affordable only to Sundance Film Festival-goers now. *Scrooges* closed the same year I went away to college. Our parents' old condo had been sold and resold for three times what they bought it for. And although my dad would have liked to join the truly wealthy set that now lived on the Park City-side of Guardsman's, we hoped the ashes winded their way back toward Brighton, the ski resort where Dad taught us to ski. He taught each of us. He packed our boots for us. He loaded the car with the skis. He skied backwards, his skis making a V with the backs as we made a V with their tips. His skis locked against ours, we made perfect S curves down the hillside, a teleological fall.

The earth's crust is the skin of the apple, the skin of a peach. Near the top, the crust is like cold wax. It crumbles, but the part nearer the mantle moves like hot wax. It shapes and reshapes. It can't premeditate or predict, but it can reform.

When I touch anyone, here in Salt Lake, my daughter or my husband or my mother, my sisters, all I get is static. They said that during the dustbowl, people in Oklahoma refused to shake hands. It was so dry there, the particles in the air so charged, so full of near mass, so full of potential energy, that a mere touch could send someone jumping a foot back. Here, it's a gentler shock but one that makes you re-think your motivations. Is it really worth it—shaking the hand, giving the kiss, patting the shoulder—knowing you're both going to suffer a jolt? But touch we do because that's what we do. The inevitable slog, the inevitable reach, the inarguable gravity. The need to touch sits somewhere on the scale between the physical need to drink water and the psychological perceived-need to drink alcohol. It's all desire and slake. All promise and quench. When your glass is empty, you ask that it be filled up. If your hand is empty, you extend it to be shaken or held or turn it upside down like a cup and let someone fill it with jelly beans or quarters or water enough to seep through the fingers, out the ridges, to puddle in the bottom of the palm. The shock doesn't hurt that badly. If you keep touching, you get used to it. Other shocks become submerged like sand at the bottom of a land-locked sea. Eventually, the shocks settle into ground, leaving you something you can build on.

Shift Your Scale

The first rule of a geologist navigating territory upon which a dam will be built is to distinguish the fault line from the bathtub ring left behind by a one-time inland sea. The second rule is to test the soil to see what structure may hold, what concrete may sink. The third rule is to remember that rock and dirt pretend to be hard and permanent lines, but over time they are as fluid as water. Have an evacuation plan.

I love Portland, Oregon, more than any place in the world. Rain makes green more possible and resistance to growth impossible. Drop a lettuce seed in the dirt on a late May morning, have a salad by that first week in June. Tomato plants reach five feet tall, the vines never needing to stop to develop a tomato to reproduce. They grow skyward forever. Western redcedars climb two-hundred, three-hundred feet tall, sometimes at a rate of two feet a year. Mushrooms grow in forests, in lawns, and in apartment carpets. The earth recycles everything—vines take down fences. Lichen dismantle fallen douglas firs. Concrete foundations need to be re-sealed, re-poured, and reinforced against the mud taking its place back.

In Portland, everyone recycles. Separate paper from plastic, take your bottles back to the store for the five-cent deposit. Taking bottles back to the Safeway, hauling two shopping carts of brown and green glass, smelling like a brewery myself, taking care not to lose a single bottle, not wanting to make a mess, not wanting to lose the nickel, I waited in line for the deposit guy to chuck my returns into his even larger barrels. He didn't mind if the bottles shattered and cracked. He counted loosely, not caring if he lost or added an extra nickel. I made enough money that time to buy a keg for a party.

> Moments after the San Fernando earthquake of 1971, only a thin dirt wall stood between 80,000 people in the San Fernando Valley of southern California and 15 million tons of water poised behind a heavily damaged dam. The 142-foot-high Lower San Fernando Dam was perilously close to failure.
> *http://earthquake.usgs.gov/learn/publications/la-damstory/*

I love Oregon and that's why I have to leave.

My boyfriend Jonathan has applied to graduate school to get his PhD in physics. He applied to all the usual places, University of Washington, Duke, CalTech. Like when Andy applied to get his doctorate in English, I applied for graduate school in all the same places.

If I had hoped that moving away from home would teach me how to make my own path separate from my father's, I was wrong. Or instead of following my father's path, I followed Andy's, then Jonathan's, with a little drinking as a compass to keep following my dad's map.

Jonathan got in to two schools—University of Washington and University of Utah. I got in to two as well—Mills and the University of Utah. I am happy. I can't believe our good fortune that we both got into the same school. Utah flies Jonathan out to visit—one of the benefits of becoming a grad student in the sciences rather than the humanities. I go with him, paying my own way.

We stay at my sister's house. She's getting married again. She's only 23 and this is her second marriage. She too, I gather, is looking for a different way although I don't approve of this one. Maybe because I think she's too young. Maybe because Jonathan and I went to Valerie's first wedding together and now will be going to her second. It seems apparent that Jonathan is not about to marry me.

On our visit, I take him out to the Great Salt Lake because no one wants to go there. It smells like salt and sulfur. It smells like rotting fish but there are no fish, just brine flies and brine shrimp.

I point out Stansbury Island. Antelope. I show him the fault lines etching a perfect compass-made circle into the foothills. The faults look just like bathtub rings from here.

Jonathan is not impressed. Compared to Portland, this place looks dead.

The valley reminds him of an old, dying man—his skin dry and flaky, his organs desiccating, his bones shrinking.

I see it through his eyes. One puff and the whole mirage of anima blows away on the static electric, smog-filled air. The more recent additions to Utah's industry, like medical technologies, brew pubs and million-dollar house constructions that sit on the fragile crust will crumble away into the pit of what the Mormons would consider rapture. MagCorp sits next to the lake. It speeds the lake toward oblivion by dumping magnesium and mercury into the already mineral-heavy lake.

In Portland, a thousand kinds of green show up in the spring— the rubbery green of rhododendron leaves, the unfurling green of fern, the shaky green of cedar needles, the pinking green of dogwood, the bent green of calendula, the sharp green of artichoke. But in Utah, the green always seems misplaced. The names of green things are usually transplanted, foreign ones—Kentucky bluegrass, Virginia Creeper, English Ivy, London Plane Tree, cheat grass— probably because early pioneers imported most of the green. Sagebrush, Utah's original green, is really more a kind of blue.

In Portland, skies mottled gray, egg-shell gray, steel gray or concrete gray deliver see-through rain, blue rain, river rain, ocean rain to make all the variations of green. To make a dust-brown bowl green, someone has to intervene to turn the color. You have to invoke some kind of transubstantiation. A body this brown doesn't transform by simple cloud. Every year it snows five hundred inches deep of hard packed snow in the mountains. Press that snow flat. Tunnel through from ground to pipe. Box it up and mail it via reservoir to the postage stamp-size lawns that square every block and carpet this bowl man's. Drink it up, Kentucky Blue. You are God's garden of blade, shallow, knotted root. You are the thirstiest of grasses. You long for the shade of your southern roots, the promise of monsoon. We'll bring you monsoon in glasses of steel, concrete and PVC.

There is so nothing that screams fertile in the Salt Lake valley, except perhaps the families with eight or nine children. The valley itself might whisper something like "water me," but that's more of a plea than a shout. If you want fierceness of fecundity, you've got to go somewhere else. But, if there's part of you that likes squeezing out an existence the same way you squeeze out a splinter—with a lot of pressure, precision and pain—then Salt Lake City is the place for you. And not just for you in the Pioneer-let's-eke-out-a-living,-dredge-the-water-from-the-hills-and-park-it-in-a-reservoir-until-we-can-all-flush,-flush,-flush-our-troubles-away way, but in the way that there is an economy, although based mostly on mineral extraction and tourism. And those things dry up. As the pumps drain the oil and the water from under the thin desert floor, the skiers slide down the mountain, pressing the snow flat, ironing the snow into one finely knit shawl. It's just lace holding this ecosystem together. The water is pressed down further. It's drunk by more and more of the children of those fertile women. The smog hangs heavily. The concrete warms the snow. The snows melt earlier. They stop coming sooner.

> Throughout earthquake-prone regions of the United States, scientists record ground motion during strong earthquakes. By studying these records, scientists can estimate the severity of shaking that is likely to occur during future earthquakes.

Jonathan has decided against the University of Utah. I have mostly decided that I'll postpone graduate school. After I go on a short visit to check out Mills' graduate school, I get back and tell Jonathan that I think I'll move with him to Seattle. Who wants to leave the fertile Pacific Northwest? When is the last time I broke up with a guy because of something as unlikely as a career in writing? We go out for drinks with our friend Rachel to celebrate our impending move.

Rachel and I go over to the jukebox to choose a song. Rachel, who hasn't seen me alone since I got back from visiting Mills, tells me that I should maybe ask Jonathan where he was last Friday. I don't want to ask him. Rachel says she has to take off. I don't want to ask him but he's right there with a pool stick in his hand, looking like he could care less if I am there, or if I am Rachel, or if I am some other girl he apparently slept with last Friday when I was out of town. I cry; he listens. All he says is, it was a slip-up. I just slid into bed with her. He doesn't ask for forgiveness.

I loved the northwest and that's why I had to leave. It was time to say no. At least to something.

I had to draw the line somewhere, eventually. The morning after Jonathan told me about the woman he'd accidentally slept with, I sent my acceptance letter to Utah.

The design of the new Los Angeles Dam is a case in point. In studying records of strong shaking from the 1971 shock and other shocks, U.S. Geological Survey (USGS) scientists realized that shaking near the epicenter of an earthquake is much stronger than had been recognized previously. Hence, they recommended the new dam be designed to withstand shaking about three times stronger than that assumed in design studies prior to USGS consultation.

If you don't measure just right. . . .

You work so hard to measure and maintain. Just one glass. Two won't kill anyone. If the neighbors were over, we'd have put that box of wine to sleep. You're a little disappointed in yourself that there's still a bit of heft to the box. You opened it yesterday. You used to be able to drink like a fish. Or more realistically, you're a little disappointed in yourself to find there's so very little left, just a drizzle. You drink just like a fish. You opened the box yesterday. One and a half liters of cold, cheap chardonnay flushing your cheeks red. Who is to say how much wine was really in that box? Your wife drank some. Maybe your kids stole a little. Maybe the wine manufacturer never filled it up all the way. Maybe you opened it a few days before. Maybe yesterday looks a lot further away than it did five years ago, than last year, maybe, in the year 1983 and gallon jugs of Gallo have gone the way of bell-bottoms and moustaches and you're on the cutting edge of technology if not oenology. You've heard of experiments where someone left a box of chardonnay in the fridge for six months and testified that that six-month-old glass of wine tasted as good as the first. You weren't sure how he could remember taste over so many long months. You also weren't sure if bagged wine by the box was meant to be anything but drunk quickly.

I had a dad. He drank like a fish. He drank like a fish in a city that has no water. If the word irony was enough to untangle, I would use that word. But it's more complicated than that. If it was easy enough to clarify: we lived in the one state whose majority population derided all things alcoholic, as alcohol was unnatural, unseemly, immoral, but delighted in greening an entire desert valley by aqueduct, channel, and reservoir from the mountain streams; therefore my family drank a lot. But that makes no sense. Causality is never irony. If one could just undo: water from mountain stream to kitchen faucet, re-formed—good. Water to wine, transformed—not so good. But words neither do nor undo.

Could I expect Jonathan to move here? To understand the crushing history of the Great Basin, Utah's drinking laws, Lake Bonneville, the Colorado Plateau, or my dad? This place will grind you into salt if you're not careful. Jonathan measured wisely and stayed in the soft soil land of the northwest. I went back to crush and grind.

The Los Angeles Dam, designed to withstand severe shaking anticipated by USGS scientists, remained intact during the Northridge earthquake. In contrast, the Lower San Fernando Dam, which was built to lower shaking standards and with 1912–1915 construction methods, suffered major damage during both the 1971 and 1994 earthquakes.

Jonathan and I broke up a couple of months after we each moved to different places. My moving back was saying no. To Jonathan. To cheating on. To following. But also to a place that I loved. I had to leave Portland. Maybe because it was too easy there—all that water. All that green. No constant reminders of my dad. A job where drinking was rewarded. Or maybe because I had to go home where although there the ground shook, I knew the ground. I could understand where to begin to lay the concrete for foundation.

It was not until I moved out of state, then back, that I understood proportion. Not everyone drinks. Some people never drink. They're neither Mormons nor Baptists nor Muslims. They just don't do it. It doesn't occur to them.

In Utah, I don't drink more. I don't drink less. I normally drink three glasses of wine a day. Sometimes, my skin flushes. Sometimes I get a headache. Three might be a lot but it seems to be in equilibrium. It's a sustainable amount of liquor. It hedges shifting soil against reinforced concrete. It balances water pressure with curvature. But in Salt Lake City, Utah, the risks weigh heavily in my hands, like mineral-heavy lakes. A lake so full of stuff it's almost rock.

Now that I'm back in Utah, I have recycling troubles. I stand at the sink with a milk carton in my hand. I have to save water. The reservoirs are low. I can't wash out the container just to recycle it.

After half an hour of standing there, I call for the dog, rip open the cardboard and let her lick out the leftovers. I stick the now clean carton in the bin and prepare a bath for myself, to luxuriate in the water I just saved.

Change

My mom stretches one leg out in front of her on the floor of her 3rd floor walk-up apartment. She bends over it, arm out-reaching ballerina style. She stretches the other side so as to not be uneven. With her other hand, she sips from her ice-cube stacked glass of chardonnay. We've just come home from eating Indian food and she's claiming that she and I are just alike.

"We observe. It's observation that furthers society."

I wonder how either of us has furthered society in any way by looking.

"It's science," she argues. "By observing phenomena, you develop insight. Insight. It's what we do. Your sister, she's all drama and ambition. She didn't used to be but here she is, not showing up again because she found people better than us to hang out with."

"Not better. Just more likely to forward her career. She gets the best of both worlds—ambition for her job and drama for us."

"We're all dramatic."

"But not at all scientific. We think Val is being ambitious and dramatic so we observe that she stood us up tonight because doing so would forward her career and make us worry about her. But maybe she was just out for drinks with her friends and blew us off."

"That's what I'm saying. We're observant."

"And the facts fit just like we told them to."

"We didn't make her stand us up."

"And maybe she's not as ambitious as we'd like to think."

Gold-colored Christmas decorations are scattered all over the floor. Some have found their way back to their cardboard boxes. I have no idea where she keeps all this stuff when it's not the holidays. Gold-leafed China that we never use sits on shelves around the fire-place. The whole house radiates—the gold carpet, the decorations, the China, the chardonnay. My mother is very good at a theme.

"True scientists let observations guide them. Let the observations lead. Let the facts speak."

"This was my favorite Christmas ever." She changes the subject. This is her newest gift—an ability to let things go. She doesn't harp on the data. She doesn't count the ice cubes or the number of glasses. She doesn't consider my glass of red. She doesn't consider where my sister really was tonight. A lack of observation can guide as well.

~ ~ ~

While we're in Salt Lake over break, the Utah Environmental Congress has invited me to an unveiling of a landmark study on the effect climate change may have on Park City's snowpack by 2030, 2070, and beyond. In traditional, cheerful-holiday fashion, they promise the night will not be full of doom and gloom. Although the talk will address the just-in results that suggest that Thanksgiving and spring break snows will be no longer, thereby losing some of the big money-making skiing days, and that the snow will likely fall more as rain, and the prediction that the ski season will shrink to a mere sixty days, they promise that THE GOOD NEWS IS WHAT THE SKI AREAS AND YOU ARE/CAN DO TO MAKE PARK CITY A LEADER IN CUTTING GREEN HOUSE GASES. I would love to learn more but my flight heads out the morning of the unveiling and in any event, it has just begun to snow. Today is not global warming day.

~ ~ ~

The Cadillac is in the garage. The front-end of the driver's side is wrinkled up like an accordion. The cold air and the smell of tossed oil hit my nose. I close the door and go back upstairs to bed. By the time I wake up again, a tow-truck has wound the Cadillac to its winch. Two policemen walk down the sidewalk away from the house.

My sister is yelling at my dad. Val has just finished the 8th grade where DARE and MADD reign supreme.

"What if it had been a person rather than a light pole?"

My dad can affect a very sad face. Sometimes it's sad because there's mustard in the corner of his mouth. Sometimes it's sad because when he slurs his words the slurs ripple through the fat of his cheeks. Sometimes it's sad because his eyelids get heavy and his bottom lip thickens. His chin juts out like he's trying to keep all the humiliations on its tip to keep from falling all over the floor, or back into his mouth where he'd have to swallow and admit them to himself like vertebrae to a spine. He shakes his head but doesn't say anything. He can barely remember light poles, let alone people.

~ ~ ~

The waste of this world (Utah) wends its way to another (Addis Ababa). The Snows of Kilimanjaro have gone like the cliché "come hell or high water." The already-thin cattle go north looking for grass. As cattle follow grass. As grass follows water. As water follows itself to the salty ocean. The salty ocean gets closer. The grass is plankton and the cattle are fish. I took a boat all the way from the Great Salt Lake to Lake Naivasha.

In Kenya we called a summit to request that the more developed nations in the world do something about their production of greenhouse gases before their country is plunged into ever-more drought. The summit to request that someone do something—stop driving their cars, watching their TV's, leaving on their lights, heating their homes, making their plastics—is a lot like a conference to do nothing. Just stop and maybe we will be able to feed our cows a little bit longer. Just stop and maybe our wells will run with a bit of water. But the we doesn't understand the they of the water. It is raining in Portland. It is raining in Michigan. It is snowing in Salt Lake. It is flooding in New Jersey. It is flooding in Louisiana. It is flooding in Texas. It is snowing in Texas and what is all this business about warm globes? We agree to meet in the high desert. We agree to bring the bottled water to the conference room. They'll bring the salt.

~ ~ ~

In a just and orderly world, my dad would have been given martinis when he was ten, beer at five. For school lunch, Bloody Marys for all. In class, his math teacher would lean against the blackboard, the chalk dust doing more than his own inner ear to stabilize him. The sine and the cosine are mocking the teacher so my dad has to stand up and explain the derivation. To him, sober one, uniquely sober man, stands up in front of the mostly-drunk class and suggests to them that rendering the quadratic formula thusly would be more elegant and that he has had some ideas of late on Fermat's Last Theorem. Or perhaps he would sit down and finally feel he was among his people. He'd take a drink. Suggest they try a Bloody Mary made with bourbon rather than vodka. Maybe he'd be of the royalty of drunkards where limousines would cart him to bars as elegant as the quadratic formula rendered thusly.

~ ~ ~

If Salt Lake were the paradise that Joseph Smith might have imagined, the Doctrine of Covenants of the Book of Mormon section—where the edicts against drinking alcohol and hot drinks reside—would not have taken such prominence in the follower's practices. To Joseph Smith, they were an afterthought. Had Smith not been shot in Illinois, the Mormons might not even have made it to Utah. Or maybe they would have come to Utah but with Joseph Smith, his chewing tobacco and his brandy snifters. A brewery would have been part of the co-op and for a couple yards of hemp and a bushel of corn, Smith would trade a barrel of his finest brew. Water would be transformed from life-sustainer to life-elixir. Beer could serve the dual purpose of quenching thirst and knitting the bonds of community more tightly. The beer, naturally antiseptic, would put those Mormon-killing bugs to rest—like a seagull to a locust. The town would grow more rapidly and people would come from afar to praise the Rocky Mountain water that percolated through the town's taps and draughts. Joseph Smith would be revered not only for founding a religion but a whole western economy based on the good news of cold beer. Perhaps he would call it Denver.

In Smith's eyes, the valley should not be forthwith carpeted with the green lawn. No, the water shall be reserved for more pertinent interests than grass. The church will build the viaduct, irrigate the land, but for a more central, more useful, more salubrious goal: keeping everyone's pints filled to the brim. In a utopian community where everything is shared—the beer, the linens, the wives—water is much too scarce to be treated as anything but the economy that it is. Beer makes water a commodity. With a price sticker on the bottle, you shall not just open the pint to pour it on the ground.

~ ~ ~

It's a desiccated mess this Valley, this liver. Alcohol saps the liver and the kidneys of their purifying power. Drinking liquor is a dehydration process and by the time you're done your body reads raisin, prune, beef jerky. Underneath all that grass is dirt so hard, so clayful, not even Prometheus could marry water with earth to make skyward-eyed man. The grass, like the pink pigment of the skin, will be the first to go. When the snow stops falling, the grass will shrink back and reveal its sterile red. And the liver. After too much insult and too many assaults, it exacts its revenge by flooding the skin with its discretion of yellow bile—the dirt is a yellow skin.

~ ~ ~

My mother does not count her drinks. My sisters and I are always noting exactly if three glasses is half a bottle and how many calories are in each glass and then, after the second, we lose count along with care, but before that, there's a whole show of moderation. My mother moderates with ice cubes. Sometimes, in the heat of summer, twelve cubes to the glass. Does she really like her wine so cold or is this some essay into the more modest realm of measure?

~ ~ ~

My mother does not count her drinks but she does count her bathrooms. My mom, with my dad, had a house in Park City before Park City started desperately calling for snow. They would rent the house out most of the time but once in awhile we would go up for ski holidays or Autumn Aloft to see the hot air balloons take off. We woke up before dawn in the morning. The whole family ducked out of the house. Under the cover of darkness we walked down the streets of Park City, past resort properties and five million dollar houses. No one walks in the suburbs of Park City. My mom carried a picnic basket. We made it to the field where the balloons lay deflated next to their baskets. My dad spread the blanket out and we all sat to watch the balloons pull up the sun. The day is all sky and movement. There is no flattening rain, no snow to send us home.

~ ~ ~

My mother has stopped complaining that she once owned nine bathrooms. There were five at the Park City house, four at our regular house. It's not that she's okay with the two bathrooms she owns now; it's that she no longer needs to belabor the point. She's stopped going to dinner with us for the most part because we're too loud and we don't cut our salad into bites small enough to fit elegantly into our mouth, but now she has us cook at her house where the ice cubes are plentiful, the cost is less and the food is much, much better. She flatters us.

She also refuses to buy good knobs for her oven, so cooking at her house is always an extra challenge: Is that burner on? I think so. Shit, this back one was on and I just grabbed the pan. If you press this one while you're turning, it will come on a little bit. We can simmer the curry there.

~ ~ ~

Superfluous. Superfluidity. Super-fertile. In the suburbs, on the foothill benches, in the historic old homes, the parents flood the rooms with children. Five, six, seven. Sometimes each with their own bathroom. They can all pee and flush simultaneously—a prayer to God who is bountiful. This bounty of toilet is for you. This bounty of green grass and seven loads of wash and six runs of the dishwasher and the sprinklers running at noon. For the bounty of car wash and roses. For the bounty of hosed down sidewalks. This bounty of swimming pools and twenty-minute showers. Of alfalfa for cows and of reservoirs for fish.

~ ~ ~

But whatever mountain moat surrounds, the valley can't keep all new ideas out. First the skiers came. And then the pagans and the hippies. In certain parts of Salt Lake, you'll see yards made out of desert—yucca and yarrow and other stick-like plants. In the tanks of some toilets you'll see bricks to keep the flow low, shower heads on timers, people washing their cars on the lawns. You might see rain-saving tanks and gray-water reclamation tubs. You might see, even in the far-removed suburbs, a few rose bushes replaced by, well, nothing; the rose garden of our old house has been concreted over to make room for an extra car.

~ ~ ~

We can be louder at my mom's apartment than at a restaurant. Two bathrooms is plenty even when my sister, her husband, her two kids, my husband and kid, my sister and her fiancé and my mom and her boyfriend are there, waiting for Valerie and I to please get the samosas on the table. We don't sit at the table at her house anymore. She puts a big blanket down on the floor, so all of us can sit, eat panak paneer, chicken curry, and drink a glass of wine, with or without ice cubes. Even if you spill these days, she has a super-powered spray she uses on the carpet. Presto. All clean. After dinner, my mother stretches her legs out in front of her and asks us exactly how it is that assisted suicide isn't an option in Utah. I tell her it is in Oregon. She promises to make me take her there if she starts to get too demented. We all laugh and ask her how we'll know too is too. She tells us we'll know. She pretends she doesn't want to live forever but she knows as well as I do that she who lives the longest gets to be noted for change, gets to fall down gracefully, gets to make the most proclamations, gets to observe the history of her choice and claim it as true.

Where the Wild Things Are

Hoping to raise a well-adjusted kid makes you think maybe establishing a few rules for yourself is a good idea. If you expect your kids to have limits, perhaps so should you. My dad. His only limit was pressing against the dominant, abstinent, Mormon culture. All that did was turn his once-hard body to mush. When I think of my dad, I don't think oil. I don't think diamond. I think deliquesce. Perhaps there are healthier limits—ones that don't just push against but ones that you make yourself. Lines you draw in the sand. Ways you learn to say no.

When Erik and I decided to start trying to get pregnant, I began to question everything I did, wondering, should I make a new rule? Should I lock the doors in the day and the night? Should I walk around naked? Can I drink wine before five or should I drink never again?

When I did get pregnant, rules were forced on me. No drinking. No sushi. No deli meats. No heavy lifting. Perhaps this is the way parents are indoctrinated into the society of good parenthood, but these rules chafed. Self-imposed rules are much easier to follow than those imposed from without. But maybe that's because those self-imposed rules bend in ways those imposed rules hold steadfast.

Maybe building dams is a good thing: hydroelectric power, water storage, flood control. Maybe they're not: canyon destruction, fish habitat destruction, earthquake hazard. A good vetting of where you plan to build, on what soil you find stable, and a careful analysis of what lies below will give you some indication of whether this is a good idea or not.

Whether or not having kids means you have to make some hard and fast rules or whether or not dams need to be built, you must first determine what the baseline for normal is, what kind of soil you're working with. When you're formed of muddled soils yourself, it's hard to begin to distinguish. But you've got to draw the line somewhere. You must first have a threshold before you can charge trespass. You have to know what's real ground and not just a fantasy of packed sand. It's up to you to investigate the strata.

Formations

We watch closely as the dog licks the baby. We think Cleo is a quarter wolf. Cleo, who lives with and loves four cats. Cleo, who thinks she's a Chihuahua and climbs into my lap when my friend's one-quarter wolf dog comes over to play. Cleo, who my mother-in-law says is a cartoon dog trapped inside a real dog's body. She'd never hurt anyone—real, cartoon, imagined, or quarter. We think. As we watch her lick the baby. As we tell her to leave the baby alone.

Things scare me. I'm afraid of running the lawn mower over my toes. I can imagine the whip of the blade as it whacks its grass-green dull edge through the pink, then red, then white of the skin, then flesh, then bone of my toes. I'm afraid I'll drop the baby from the bed when I tug the blanket out from under her when I'm cold at night. I'm afraid I won't get a job and have to declare bankruptcy; I'll miss a grant deadline and shut down the magazine; that the Supreme Court will be stacked with strict constructionists that decide the amendments—especially one through ten—aren't really part of the constitution; that the airplane will crash; that the car heading east will not see the stop sign nor my north-running car; that I'll offend my mother by telling her her bridge group seems slightly medicated.

But these are easy, modern fears. These kinds of fears substitute for real fear. These fears are easily mollified with modern fixes—

vascular surgery for the toe, a credit line of $40,000, bankruptcy laws, a Supreme Court that will turn over under a different administration, assurances that all babies fall off the bed at least once and live, that planes rarely, rarely crash, cars usually stop at stop signs, and my mother gets mad at the dumb things I say a lot and then forgives me a lot.

These fears—are they holdovers from the time when lions chased us? When the flight or fight response meant more than driving really fast after flipping off the SUV that cut you off on the freeway. Are these holdovers from the time when the buffalo kicked one last kick an inch away from your tender, Neanderthal skull as you plunged the tip of the spear further in? Is lying in bed awake at night, wondering if you forgot to put the car in park, to put a stamp on the bill, to lock the door, just a residue of watching the cave you call home flood? All the beans you'd stored for winter are lost. Without those beans, you know you're going to starve.

Caveman feared nature because nature usually trumped him. Now that we have wrested nature into our control, our fears have likewise transformed. Nature itself, barring hurricane and earthquake, stands still and submissive outside our doors. As we sit inside the comfort of our homes, in the warmth of our blankets and the crispness of our sheets, we lie in bed fearing not nature, but nature perverted. And the more that nature is twisted to suit our desire, the more perverted our natures become.

There are two fears that I think of as real—the threat of nature becoming completely obliterated and all things wild, especially predators, made extinct, and some "pervert" molesting my daughter. But within human nature and out in the natural world, there's a country of mutations, & transformations & civilizations— nature's not necessarily pure and not necessarily nice. But then, neither is what we do to it. In the mix of acting and being acted upon, it's impossible to even distinguish what is natural and what is a perversion of that nature. These two fears—the absence of predators, the proximity of predators—funny how they materialize, mostly via fantasy.

The First Fantasy

She feels his hot breath behind her. She clutches her basket tighter. She outruns the wolf only to find him at her grandmother's house. He seems so safe there—domesticated. When she takes off her cloak she is revealed. When she takes off her cloak, she reveals him in the way he looks at her: "what big eyes you have," the way he smells her: "what a big nose you have." Everything is large. The wolf is huge in comparison to the little girl. The wolf measures his body against hers—every feature of his maleness, his wolfness, dwarfs her. It's a struggle but somehow he manages to get his way into her little basket. Red Riding Hood, disrobed, is still red all over.

The hunter kills the wolf by filling the wolf's belly with rocks. When he stands up, he falls over. His hardness kills him. But now Little Red Riding Hood is trapped alone in the cabin with another lonely, large beast.

What is the role of the Little Red Riding Hood? Why is her basket a double entendre? How did it come to be that the words red riding hood came to be a euphemism for clitoris? Why did she go walking in those old woods alone? Little Red Riding Hood has a job to fulfill, a role to play. No matter what color her hood or her cloak, she'll still be left in the backwoods cabin first with a wolf, then with a lonely old hunter. Little Red Riding Hood was born defenseless and with a juicy little body. Who's to say she isn't the most natural prey around?

Pink Cliffs

The ultrasound moves over my stomach. A projection of the contents of that stomach is beamed up against the wall as if we were at a drive-in theater. We see a heart, a liver, two kidneys. All the parts seem to be in their proper place except for one. I keep looking for the tell-tale sac. I search for something dangling between the legs. The fetus turns over; we see a cute bum and two fleshy melon slices. And the radiologist announces it's a girl. She types it single-handedly on the computer's keyboard. She hits return and the baby is branded. She's a girl.

I can't stop crying. I was so sure it would be a boy. How could it be a girl? I've known so many girls. I am a girl.

Erik cannot understand. It's a healthy baby. Who cares what the sex is?

I can't stop crying. I want to hide. I want them to check the scan one more time. Please I say. Please, I finally say aloud. Please God, I say to Erik, the world is so much harder for girls.

I don't mean to brand my baby a victim. She's not. She's strong. But unlike Erik who believes he can, I don't believe I'll be able to protect her, to watch out for her every step of the way. At some point, she'll be on her own. I will give her the tools I can and then wish her luck when the man in the van pulls up alongside her as she rides her bike. Or, more likely, when the boy next door comes over to help her fix that bike. Alone. In the garage. Or her cousin wants to play truth or dare. Or her brother wants to move his room downstairs, next to hers. Or the man across the street asks her to come help him find his kitten. How do I teach her to draw the line when talking to strangers when I don't know where to draw it myself?

At ten years old I was already looking for someone to see me, smell me, understand me differently. Of course my parents loved me. That wasn't the trouble—they were born to love me. The trouble was, I wanted to see if I could get someone other, outside our family, to see what I was like on the inside. I meant it as metaphor. The boy took it literally.

Grey Cliffs

As he aims at the wolf, he imagines he's protecting his livelihood, his family's financial security, maybe even their physical security. Well, at least the physical security of his cattle. Which, in some ways, until he sends them off to the stockyard, he thinks of as family. He can't stand to hear calves cry. It reminds him of his daughter—the way she cries from nightmares. He thinks she has an overactive imagination. He tells her not to watch so much TV. When his wife goes to their daughter in the middle of the night, he can't quite rouse himself from bed. He turns on his side and looks through the open window at the once sage-covered land. His cattle range there. Cheatgrass has replaced most of the sage and nearly all the perennial grasses. The cheatgrass is harder on the cattle's stomach than the native grasses. But it grows where they do. Like the cow, it claims its territory as its own wherever it goes.

The rancher imagines a wolf standing on the farthest hill. The wolf waits for his pack. The pack circles around the calf. The calf cries for its mother. The rancher can't save the calf. But he can save the cow. From where he lies in bed, he closes one eye. He focuses his other eye through the imaginary scope of his long barreled rifle.

Is the fantasy of the wolf worth the life of one cow? Is keeping the fantasy of *the wild* intact worth the potential loss of even a hundred cattle, or, rather, one hundred cattle at seven-hundred dollars a head? Where do you draw the line? Six hundred wolves, six, none?

I am outside of Utah, southwest of Yellowstone State Park. I've left our big black husky Cleo home with Erik and am on my way to camp by myself for the first time. I have our lightest tent and our warmest sleeping bag. I am six months pregnant and following my mother-in-law's steps to find out what my familiar animal is, my totem, to find out what the baby's might be. Go into the woods, she said, and draw a big circle around the camp. Whichever animal crosses the boundary of your circle first is your familiar. I decide to get out of Salt Lake to draw my circle and head toward less past-saturated ground by heading to Wyoming. My mother is from Wyoming. Perhaps I should press on to Idaho. But I don't think I have enough snacks, or enough balls, really, to stay away another day, which is how far Idaho is, now that I'm this far north.

The map lies open on the passenger seat but I think I've passed the turn-off to the campsite I'd picked for its relative isolation yet proximity to the road in case I chicken out and decide to bail in the middle of the night. I wish I was braver but I don't sleep well even at home, each noise—a cat bringing in a mouse, the dog jumping off the couch, Erik walking across the floor—startles me awake. I wonder who is trying to get inside our house and what they may want. They could steal my lap top, my wedding ring, but I've seen enough movies to know that what they really want is to tie my husband up and rape me while they make him watch. I know he would never recover.

This close to the road, I can fear both human and animal predators. Once, on another camping trip, I'd scared away a bear before by singing Don McLean's "American Pie"—probably bored him to death with all fourteen verses, or drove him mad by the off key of my singing voice—but that was in Oregon. In Wyoming, the wild seems more wild and more fraught—bears, cougars, wolves are hungrier in the desert mountains. I also worry about weird men, combing the highways, looking for wayward women who are looking to find themselves before they are irrevocably changed into that heavy word, mother. I do not think I have my mother-in-law's sensibility. Her head hits the pillow at night and she's out like a light bulb—just like her son. Her familiar probably just walked right up to her calm self and brushed her shoulder as it walked passed. My likely familiar is a grasshopper or an empty can of Diet Coke.

Now I'm two-hundred miles from home and committed to try to stay. I pull the tent and the sleeping bag out of the car. I distract myself by gathering firewood and thinking about how to make dinner on the campfire without attracting bears. I decide to cut the meat into squares and grill my steak on a stick and eat it right off the skewer. The smell on the wind from the ten minutes it takes to sear may tickle a bear's nose, but it won't last long enough or be strong enough to persuade him to walk all the way past the river and down to the road.

I'm obsessed with the idea of a bear crawling into my space, invading my circle. I'm distracted from my dinner as I keep looking up from my stick and out into the woods. As my teeth rip through the sinewy steak, I see something in the trees. I think it is Cleo the dog. Erik has come and brought the dog to protect me. But Cleo doesn't run to me. And Erik doesn't emerge from the bushes. I stop chewing. I see her black nose and silver snout. She is thin. Thinner than any dog. But bigger than my Cleo. I take my eyes off of her for one second to look behind me. I know she's probably not alone. Or maybe she is. Is this time for me to go? The signal is buried under layers of fantasy, real concern, mollification, fantasy, real concern, mollification. I can't hear the danger.

The list of what I know about wolves is short and contradictory:
They travel in packs.
The Lone Wolf.
Cleo is descended from wolves.
Cleo sits on the couch.
A pack of wolves can tear a goat into forty-four pieces in less than a minute.
A single wolf can kill a deer with one jump and twenty-six teeth.
My mother-in-law had a wolf named Tyco.
Tyco died when he caught the scent of a bitch in heat, jumped the fence and got hit by a car.
Wolves keep herds of deer healthy and strong.
Wolves eat calves and lambs. Fences can't keep them out.
Jack London would have died for his wolf.
Jack London killed his wolf for food.
This wolf, looking at me, would kill me for my steak.
If I feed her, will I be bound to her forever in my newly coined proverb that she who feeds the wolf owes it a living? Or will I have made her less wary of humans, but no less dangerous? By the same turn, will I have to convince Cleo to share the sofa or should I make her sleep on the floor?
If I feed her, will half a steak be enough or will she think my fatty legs would be fine dessert?
I can't see if the wolf moves. I can't even be a hundred percent sure it's a wolf. But just in case, I put the steak down, move away from it. I search my pants' pockets for the car keys. The sleeping bag makes it in the car. The tent does not. I drive like a bat out of hell the two-hundred miles back home. I met my familiar and I ran away. Maybe I can hear the alarm bells. Maybe I'm just a chicken.

Threshold

At home: It is a full moon. No solar or lunar eclipse threatens, but it's bright out there. My dog Cleo paces from eleven p.m. to one a.m. It is ninety degrees at midnight even with two fans and the swamp cooler running. Cleo never paces. Maybe she is sick. I make myself get up. She runs to the backdoor. She never has to pee in the middle of the night, but there's always a first time. The way she darts out the backdoor, I know there is trouble. Something sniffing around in our long dark yard. There have been moose down here this summer. It could even be a cougar. We live just a half mile away from the part of the canyon where a cougar was treed last year. A contingent of wildlife and city officials saved the cougar from hunters by referencing the city ordinance that states it is illegal for firearms to be discharged within city limits. Thank god the city limits stretch into the canyons.

So, whatever Cleo has run outside to find could conceivably be a cougar. But the sound of the animal as Cleo chases it is high and clacking. It's not a cougar. Or a moose. Or even a fox. It's the raccoons that used to come by, even come in our house to eat the cat food that I had stupidly placed right in front of the cat door. They'd come in and we would thank god in the morning that the only signs the raccoons left were some jittery felines and an empty bowl of food. I had heard stories about the way raccoons tear cats apart—how they perform surgical dismemberments of domestic cats. As I listened to Cleo sniff the perimeter, I could hear my cat Box's bell-collar ring. Cleo is scaring the raccoons. The raccoons were going to take out their panic on the cat. Or maybe they would turn and attack Cleo. Isn't that how Old Yeller died, or was it one of the dogs in *Where the Red Fern Grows*? No, that was a cougar that killed that dog.

It is one in the morning and I have to yell Cleo's name. I hope I don't wake the neighbors. I won't go back there because even though I know it's nothing too dangerous, like a cougar, I imagine (is this fantasy?) the raccoons turning their sharp claws on me—or, at the very best, mimicking the angry raccoons that once threw tomatoes at my friend Gabe as he tried to camp on what had apparently become their home. I worried for Cleo. I worried for Box. And now that I remembered Gabe's story, I worried about the survival of the tomatoes.

Cleo comes quick to my calling. She's scared the hell out of the raccoons and sent them into the shrubs. I can still hear Box's collar tingling. I hope that's not the raccoons, trophy collecting, as they cut open Box with their scalpel claws, remove his heart, his kidneys.

Box comes in an hour later—intact. He probably missed the raccoon/Cleo row entirely. I take off his cat collar and lock the cat door so he can't go back out there.

I want to say this to ranchers about wolves. Your lambs and calves will probably come home. Fantasizing about the way the wolves hunt your livestock is a waste of time. Better to spend it building fences. Bring the defenseless in the house. Lock the doors tight. It's important to maintain good boundaries between predator and prey.

But when I ask to see the rancher's home, the rancher draws with his finger in the air the boxy, notched shape of the state of Utah. We are nestled safely inside that box. It is Yellowstone that is the wild foothills. Everything consigned inside the square is relatively predator-free. Aside from tomato-throwing raccoons, we're all safe within our fenced backyards.

Second Fantasy

I dream of the wolf I saw. She has walked over a hundred miles having eaten only the three bits of steak I'd left behind. Her paws are ragged. She travels at night, for fear the ranchers will see her. She spends her days hiding under fallen trees and crevices in rock. Drinking from lakes, she sees the moon reflected in the lake. No one, no bear, no mosquito, no squirrel disturbs her. No fish disturbs the water.

She's coming to see me. I should leave the door open. I should close the door and lock it tight.

She goes by no other name. We all know her as Little Red Riding Hood, even her grandmother. This makes it easier to dissociate from her—the wolf cannot see her as a complete person—only as pretty—red with blood and life and one cotton barrier between his teeth and her young flesh. In a classic case of blame-the-victim, she has committed the ordinary sin of leaving her house and going outside, beyond her backyard, all alone. I ask, what kind of grandmother, sick or no, asks a little girl to tromp through the forest with candy or muffins or whatever. If she had some medicine, or special healing powers or even chicken soup. . . . The grandmother should have known better. As should the parents (where are they? In their house, watching TV? In their beds, trying to sleep?). The story can only take place in the fantasy of the forest—full of ferns and mushrooms and burbling brook, properly populated with lions and bears and wolves. This story, when written, couldn't have happened. The forests of Western Europe had been nearly devoid of all bears and wolves since the Middle Ages. The story means to confuse the wolf, the grandmother and Red Riding Hood. Little kids know the way nouns, and the definitions that bound them, shift.

First Step

Amy Albo was looking for a new house. She and John had decided to finally bite the real-estate bullet and move out of their downtown rental and invest in suburbia. Amy is a good—balanced, attentive, cautious, devoted—mother of two children.

Amy emailed me to ask if I knew how to scan photographs for a brochure for a writing conference we're working on. And, as an addendum, she added that, while she was house hunting, she looked up Utah's list of sex offenders. A Megan's Law that forces people convicted of sexual abuse to alert authorities of their addresses. Those addresses are posted online. Online, Amy Albo found a man who lived not only on our street, but on our block of our street. She wasn't sure of his crime. She thought, hopeful, that it may have been something minor like ordering porn. I should check out the state's official sex offender website, just in case.

When I access it, which I swore I wasn't going to do, the database overwhelms me with various names for sexual abuse. Instead of letting you punch in an address, the main web page lists all the sex crimes with the attendant violation codes.

Aside from the list of crimes, the website includes several warnings about the information—how the information is correct to some degree, how this information does not necessarily imply the offender will commit this particular crime in the future and how you're not supposed to harass or stalk the offender. That's not the point of the website, they seem to be insisting. I'm unsure exactly what the point is then—to convince people not to move within a thousand feet of him? A thousand blocks? To keep their children locked indoors at all times?

But I'm curious. I'm worried. I'm pregnant. This is something I suppose I ought to know. I think of our neighbors. Evelyn on the corner lives alone, Margot, who drives a black Forester, is recently divorced and lives with her two young kids. Matt and Jenn are our age and are xeriscape gardeners. That doesn't mean anything. On the corner is a dad of four whose main crime is wearing a mullet and warming up his new Ford 150 diesel for an hour on cold mornings. Two guys—father and son, I believe, live down on the corner. They've covered their yard in red lava rocks. Perhaps they may be worrisome, but at least they're three houses down. Next is the lesbian and her female tenants and next door to us is John who salvages broken-wing birds and is an amateur archaeologist. He sifts the dirt in his front lawn, looking for treasure. His son is homeschooled and seven years old. I doubt he's been out of the house often enough to meet a kid not related to him, let alone been left alone with one. Still. It could be any of them.

I type in my zip code.

Twenty-nine offenders pop up.

One of them is on G street. Unlawful Sexual Intercourse. I'm not sure what that means, but I can't imagine it's more than having sex with a minor, or, even more likely, in Utah, it means he was caught having sex with a man. Or even receiving oral sex. I exhale. I discount these charges to be born of a hyped up "we legislate morality" culture.

But I browse too quickly. My eye finds our address. No, wait. Not our address but the exact number of address plus three. Across the street. The new neighbors who are fat and friendly.

Apparently, the man is also a child rapist.

I sit in my front room and look at their cars. His Toyota is a Rav 4. The Nissan is parked in the driveway. They're home at strange times. All the time. The same times I'm home—which is always. I lock the door.

I call for Erik. I start to cry. I don't know what else to do.

I wish we weren't having a girl.

I look down at my stomach and suck it in. Who can I trust? At least while she's inside me, I can protect her. But what about these thoughts, traversing placenta-ways? Contaminating her. Making her nervous already. Boundary-concerned. Boundary-confused.

Erik tells me not to get so upset. That can't be good for the baby either. I go outside without my shoes on. I still don't know what to do.

White Cliffs

As soon as I began telling people I was pregnant, I started getting this feeling in my stomach that I named the woogles. My stomach gets a few butterflies and my skin chills and some kind of bug crawls up my spine.

I stop in the hallway of the English Department and Dave tells me congratulations and then asks if I'm going to nurse. He gives me the woogles.

Jeff looks at the pants' waistband and tells me I'll need new clothes—soon. I get the woogles.

I think of my dad and how he'll miss out on seeing my baby. More woogles.

Even simple questions like when is your due date and do you know if it's a boy or girl give me the woogles.

It's as if everyone can see me now on the inside. Like I've drunk a draught of barium and everyone has x-ray vision. In their eyes, I see my tendons stretch and my pelvic bones shift. They all know exactly which day Erik and I had sex. I can imagine them picturing the sex. I can imagine them imagining the sperm hitting egg. I can imagine them dividing the zygote into embryonic parts. Each time that I confirm to someone new I'm pregnant, I feel like I'm giving them something full of matter and mass, that the word "pregnant" carries its own placenta of blood and food. I hand the word over and they take my insides home with them. My insides have been outed. I am known more than biblically. They know me like God knows me—all my secrets, all my wishes, all the mass of potential as it divides inside me and then divides again. My insides are everyone's property. I try not to balk. I was taught to share. Maybe the woogles are intuition. Maybe that's where I should try to draw the line. Keep the people out of my head, if not out of my body.

Second Step

Outside, I sit on the porch steps on the side of the house. Across my front yard, across the street, I can see his Pathfinder and their front door. I imagine him leering out his front window, waiting for me to give birth. I imagine he knows it's a girl. I try to quash the picture of infant molestation. Not even the bad TV program *Law & Order: Special Victims Unit* has dared to do anything but mention, in the most cryptic, detached language, the words "when she was a baby." Or "when she was two." But still. I can extrapolate. Diaper changes. Potty training. Putting down for a nap. Babies may be the most available victims of all—because so few of us can fully imagine such a thing taking place.

I try to force myself to imagine. To think of it before it happens is to ward it off. But I can't. My mind jumps to him watching my baby when she's six, playing in the front yard. He comes over and says the nicest words in the world to her: "You're my favorite little girl on the planet. How did you get so smart? How did you get so beautiful?" To my baby, these are the words she's heard all her life and yet the words she'll spend the rest of her life hoping to hear, from someone else. From someone who is not her mother.

At nine, she's riding her bike to the park and he pulls up alongside, praising her for how fast she can pedal. Telling her to be careful. Offering her a ride home.

I can't get further than this in my imagination. I retreat back to the computer to look for more ways to ward off predators than pre-thought thoughts.

I think about putting up signs in the neighborhood to alert people to potential sexual predation. I think about calling his landlord and seeing if he knows who he has rented to. I think about going over there and confronting him, telling him that I know what he did and that I'm watching him. I imagine begging him please not to hurt anyone else, especially my daughter.

Of course, a big part of me thinks this is ridiculous. From the beginning I wonder if it's just a bit strange that Amy chose her neighborhood based on its lack of sexual predators. People move all the time. Anyone could move next door or across the street without warning. At least I know to watch him. And I have to remember that whatever "Attempted Forcible Rape of a Minor" is, it was a long time ago. Maybe it was a one-time thing. Maybe it was a misunderstanding. I want to ask him. I want to go over to his house and sit down with him and say, what happened. Have him explain how he works— why little girls? No. Just one little girl. How little?

We can't protect our children from everything, maybe anything. Being particularly vigilant, erecting every foreseeable barrier against one kind of danger just allows other kinds of danger to swamp right in.

I wonder, as I watch him carry grocery bags into his house, about how normal he looks. Maybe he is normal. Maybe everything is normal to some degree. Maybe she was thirteen. Maybe thirteen is normal. Maybe, now that I've been thinking about this too long, all the lines have blurred and I see it all as a matter of degree—statutory rape is not rape. Consent is in the mouth of the giver. I go back inside. Either way, normal will now include locking the front door.

At the same time I find this out, I'm writing letters on behalf of wolves moving into Utah. Or, rather, I'm not so much writing as thinking about writing and reading news and letters to the editor about the return of the wolf. The letters run the gamut.

The points are various: some anthropomorphize the wolf, calling him vicious. Someone responds by saying that obtaining food for survival can't be called "vicious." Others bring up the somewhat tangential history of Louis Pasteur. Some think it's ridiculous that hunters, not only ranchers, can be compensated for lost—what? Prey? Experience? Livelihood? Lifestyle? Compensated for a deer they should have been able to shoot in the woods as if all deer are human property? Perhaps, the writer suggests, we should compensate hunters for any deer we may kill on the road with our cars. One letter writer finally gets to the crux of the matter: Who pays for the wolves? If we compensate the ranchers and the hunters, the taxpayers will foot the bill. The next day, someone retorts: "Who pays for humans?" Habitat destruction, resource depletion, he writes, are expensive to restore, if not impossible. Wolves belong in nature. And then, the final letter about the nature of wolves and the nature of man:

INSTINCT IS NOT EVIL

John Anderson (Forum, June 24) complains that wolves are simply "vicious, deadly, aggressive predators in real life." I am in total agreement that wolves are deadly, aggressive predators. But vicious?

Only human arrogance (often touted as intelligence) would label animals who act on survival instincts as vicious. People kill other people for revenge, hate, spite, etc., yet wolves just want their next meal. Killing them off for trying to survive is not an option. (*SL Tribune* June 26, 2005)

Death by nature. Death by man. Still amounts to the same thing. Humans are already in the mix: we've destroyed habitat, restored habitat, killed the wolf off, brought the wolf back. Is this even the same wolf it used to be? Are these natural wolves coming in from Yellowstone, or are they some kind of sheep-killing, man-made dog grown to confirm man's worst fears?

Instinct is not evil—unless it is.

Thinking about my neighbor as a specific kind of predator, a molester, made the idea of molestation real. Through all the counseling sessions and honest divulgences to boyfriends and at Speak-Outs and in my own writing, I never really understood why my mom made such a big deal. Having had sex, having been molested, were words I used in the high-sensitivity 1990s to describe why I was who I am now or how far I've come or how I'm like every other victim of man and men. I told it like I tell a story. It had become a metaphor with such obvious associations that even though it gained me some attention, I started being sick of talking about it, defining myself by it, thinking it had anything to do with me. I staved off victimhood by telling other stories, by writing in the third person, by making poetic and empty gestures to the wind about the power of wolves. But my own daughter. That somehow made it hit home.

Fantasy 3

Maybe the wolves should stay in Yellowstone. I don't have the stomach to fight for them. Not that I have any illusion that I make any impact on the case. Hopelessness is the time Erik and I went to the Regional Advisory Council meeting to try to convince them not to raise the number of cougar permits from five-hundred and twenty to seven-hundred and thirty. Do seven-hundred and thirty cougars still live in Utah?

The high school was hot. We were in Springville. They won't have these meetings in the relatively liberal Salt Lake City for fear the animal rights nuts come out and state their blind case. Erik and I drove for miles to attend. I was the only woman there. Every one else: sportsmen and ranchers. One guy stood up to speak about his dogs. He advertised their special cougar tracking ability. If you want to hunt with him, dial 1–800-tree-a-cat. One man spoke about the imminent cougar threat to his children as they played, innocently, in their backyard. Someone else spoke about the one sheep he lost in 1997. He couldn't be sure it was cougar. Could have been coyote. But still. His sheep, his land, his birthright since 1865. No one bothered to mention to him that the cougar's ancestors pre-dated his. Most everyone was there to decry the paucity of game deer. The drought had wiped the deer population out. And who the hell were these cougars to infringe on their trophy hunt? Erik and I stumbled up to the podium. I said something particularly lame like, "how can you issue so many permits when no one has done a feasible study on how many cougars are actually out there?" There was no booing. Just rowdy talk over my voice. This wasn't a meeting to determine the number of permits. No. It was more like a poetry reading by a friend that everyone goes to and says they love because it's the nice thing to do. In addition to confirming what they all believed—that cougars in any number are that number too many. Preaching to their own choir. The way they sang. As an added bonus, each took home that handy number—1–800-tree-a-cat in magnet form for their fridge.

Vermillion Cliffs

I don't usually conceive rape fantasies, but I do think up innocence-corrupted ones. Ones like teacher seducing student, bishop seducing parishioner, doctor seducing patient. During the six months of pregnancy, before I contribute to the wilding/weirding of her sexuality by contaminating her with my non-missionary-style fantasies via the placenta, I decide to stop thinking these thoughts. I'm not entirely convinced these fantasies are bad. They make up my sexual identity. What if I don't have any sexuality after I delete these from my database of turn-ons? What if I feel like how I sometimes feel at parties without a glass of wine in my hand— like I may have no reserves to go to in order to rise to the occasion and be sociable?

But, as any drinker who binges before they dry out, I invent one more fantasy.

I (but the "I" is not really me. The female in the fantasy is usually blank-faced. So is the man for that matter) am in a church parking lot. I'd stayed late helping to teach Sunday school (I am sixteen, say). My ride had left early. As I stand around fretting, the newest member of the Priesthood (it's always more subversive to make the story about Mormons) comes out to get in to his car. His is the only car, an old Honda, left in the parking lot. It's summer and the asphalt is hot. He sees her (see how quickly I change to third person) and asks if she needs a ride. She says, sure. No reason to worry about someone moving up the ladder toward all salvation.

They had known each other, a little, in elementary school. But now he's graduated and his family is planning his mission. At 18, and as a male, he has all the authority of the church behind him. So, when he suggests taking a back route to her home, she doesn't question him.

So the clichés begin—he runs over a snake, stops the car, turns it off, and gets out to look at the snake. The snake slithers away. He gets back in the car but the car "won't start."

Things can take many turns.

One is that the guy has beer. She takes a sip. A slippery slope. Once she has a taste of liquor (against the Church's Words of Wisdom) what recourse does she have to refuse him from there?

The other is he asks her to follow him, to chase the snake or deer or rabbit or whatever he saw out of the corner of his eye.

Since it's too hot to wait in the car, he suggests they take a blanket and sit in the shade of a copse of scrub oak.

She sits down as gracefully as she can in her white (white?) dress.

He asks her what she likes best about the Bible.

She says she likes the story of the Garden of Eden.

He says, does she know that the garden is the most important part of that story? That before Eve ate, then offered the bite of the apple, Adam and Eve had sex all the time?

She says, she thought that the sex was the punishment. That the shame of their nakedness had to do with them finally coming to know each other as opposite, with opposite parts, and that's where attraction, and pain, lie. In difference.

He touches the neckline of her dress.

No, he clarifies for her. It's not difference that makes for sexual attraction; it is power.

In the garden, God had power. The garden had power. And Adam had full power over Eve. It was Eve who went out of line, and disobeyed the garden, Adam, and God.

To get into heaven, he suggests, women should obey. Preferably in a garden.

Stand up, he tells her.

She stands. She thinks they're getting ready to leave.

He stands up behind her and puts his hands on her shoulder. He unzips the top of her dress and unhooks her bra. Turn around, he tells her. She does. He pulls on the sleeves of her dress, exposing her bra. He puts his hand over her breasts and takes her bra off with the back of his hands.

Her dress hangs at her hips. Some clothes do add an element of intrigue, he agrees.

You ever done anything like this before? he asks.

She shakes her head.

It's all right. He promises. I've been blessed. Any part of me that touches you will be blessed too. The saliva in my mouth is like holy water. To prove it, he bends down to put his tongue on her breast. Now your breast is saved. He smiles.

(And then things take another turn. I become the he.)

He presses his tongue against her other breast, puts his whole mouth around it.

She startles.

Here's the tricky part, I tell her, as I push down on her shoulders, to get her to kneel. With one hand on the top of her head and one undoing the buckle and buttons of my jeans, I try to explain. First, I must be made unclean by a mouth that makes promises it doesn't keep. Then, I have to be recleansed.

Where am I? I am both the man and the woman, the predator and the prey, the top and the bottom.

I pull my penis out from the underwear and put the tip of it on her mouth. I nudge it between her lips to get me to open them, but she keeps them closed. She is me. I keep them closed but the pressure against my lips makes my mouth water.

Come now, he says, it won't hurt. Open up. You like apples so much.

I open my mouth a little, he says wider. I taste something mucousy and salty on my tongue. The taste makes me open wider.

Keep your teeth behind your lips.

I push deeper toward the back of her throat.

I almost gag but I take control. I master my cheek, my throat muscles and push him back. They fight in her mouth until he stops and says wait, I'm too close.

I tell her to lie down.

I press what is left of her dress up so now it's all bunched at her hips.

You're so sweet. You smell so sweet. She didn't expect nice words. She wonders if with salt comes sweet.

I soon learn the answer because he's nudging down my underwear. I press my legs together which makes him pull my panties harder.

Come on, he says again. I can tell you like this. We're almost there. Naked. Back to the way things should be.

I scoot the rest of her dress off and she lies there with the cold breeze running over her.

I am cold. Cold enough to arch up toward his warmth. This is wrong. This arching. He did not tell me to arch. I am not clean. I am not fruit. I am reaching. This is no longer his game.

I have to cleanse you. I think you'll like it, he says. He puts his hand on the mound of my pubes. Just open your legs a little. His hand cups me like it could lift me up, like it could make me a world unto myself, turn me into an apple. Where his hand is, finger against wet flesh, makes me obey. I press my whole hand against my vagina, like I'm cupping it to keep my hand warm. Then I tickle me with my index finger. Her legs spring open farther. In little circles, his finger moves inside her.

I put my hand on his stomach. It is the safest place.

I put my hand on her stomach. I know she can't resist the promise.

His face bends down to where his hand is. He follows the movement of his finger with his tongue. Almost clean, he mumbles.

I rise up to meet me, my seemingly gigantic penis throbbing on my stomach for a moment. Then I rock back and place the tip where his tongue was. Now, he says, my own spit will clean me.

He presses the tip of his penis into me, then moves it up and down. I'll go slow, but this may hurt a bit. If you really are clean now.

Say 'oh' when it feels good.

It takes a minute but I say 'oh' before I do.

We want always to be the actors. The noun in the sentence. The dam builders. The deer herd thinners. The jailers. But there are natures outside our control. Even inside our own.

It's all about proximity. Nature. And power too. And all the old clichés about women and youth and pretend accident.

Women want to be forced. Or seduced. Semantics?

Younger is better.

Prone to accident. Whoops! His penis just fell into me.

It's virginal to place the blame on others, to being the direct object to some man's hard noun. When something is done to you, how can you be accused of choosing, of even conspiring?

Lines in the Sand

When Erik and I started telling people that this baby is a girl, they all sympathized with Erik about the chastity belts and the midriff-showing shirts and the guns in the closet to threaten the boys bringing the girls home from dates, and Dad out at the car knocking on the windows saying, get my daughter in the house right now. Boys are the culprit. The girls are the victim—we engrave the syllogism so deeply that we don't even allow, except in our fantasies, the girl to be on top. The lecherous teacher. Our minds correct all the images of the girl making the boy bend over. If we can always count on direction—this leads that, boys fuck girls—then our fantasies separate from our actual sex lives.

But there is a subversive element to these fantasies that plays out in real life.

We ask the predator child molester to do even more than keep his fantasies separate. We want his erased. But that's as simple as asking that the direct object be the nominative noun. That's as simple as asking the cow to start chomping on the wolf.

And what of the darker fantasies—the one where the girl's pubic hair is soft down instead of wiry curls. The one where the baby's fingers wiggle so delicately inside the slippery vaginal darkness. The one where the boy's penis fits so wholly inside the mouth and the one where the girl's mouth fills so fully with the man's. No one—not the writers of *Law and Order: Special Victims Unit* or the men of NAPVA or the molestation novels of Dorothy Allison's *Bastard Out of Carolina* or *Fall on Your Knees*. No one admits to getting into the head of the fucker. But in a world where we want our actors to have volition—to choose to lure the ten-year-old over with the newest video game, to choose to eat the domesticated (off-limits) lamb instead of the (up for grabs) deer—it is we who have a hard time distinguishing between natural fantasy or the fantasy of the natural.

Chocolate Cliffs

The lamb walks alongside the ewe. The ewe packs its woolen coat tightly against the ewe to its left and the ewe to its right. Their heads bob in unison as they head down the grassy hill into the flatland of sparsely wooded aspens. The aspens divide the sheep. The aspens made a reverse loom—instead of finishing the white rug, the trees unwove the rug of sheep, separating lamb from ewe.

Perhaps if the lamb had been kept knit-tight next to its mother. Perhaps if the lamb had practiced keeping its eye out, imagining predation.

All it takes is one aspen to drop the stitch, to flick the lamb out of the weave and into the plain dirt-filled, tree-dark world.

As the wolves bite down, the lamb lifts its neck. Does the lamb fault himself for his short legs, his slow speed, the failure to heel to its mother? Or does he blame the tree, the bell, the shepherd, his mother for turning him to prey? Or does he blame the wolf, who was only waiting?

If you look at it in certain ways, I come from a family of female victims—women who were impregnated when they were fifteen by elementary school janitors across the street, left by husbands when they were eight months pregnant, widowed at fifty by mean drunks, molested by uncles, diddled by cousins, sold for a night for a bag of marijuana, hit by husbands, raped in a bathroom, molested by neighbors, sent for abortions, forced to give birth to children they couldn't keep at sixteen.

Men, from this perspective, may not be bad in general, but are bad in particular. You can see why there may be a hint of fear in these women's sweat when men come around. Why there may be a looking up as if the sky or the cloud may save them. Why there's a quiet impatience to find a way back into the herd, into the weave, muddled and milky and plain.

But, from another perspective, this victimhood has its own power. The damsel in distress. The flocking to save. The measures we will take to protect something happening to our babies. To think, "And it has to stop with me." To check the database. To choose a neighborhood dependent. To buy a gun. To raise a gun. To look at our front door as the barrier between good and evil. To say that we've done good at keeping danger at bay. As far at bay as we can draw our borders. To be able to say, I can tell the difference between predator and suitor, between wolf and dog.

But for each line that we draw, we compose a new nature. Whenever humans impact nature, whether on psyches—like pedophiles creating pedophiles—or changing habitat or changing the food chain, we establish new borders, new dams, new ways for the water to flow. And this nature, we think we can keep in check. We can keep nature the thing we do things to. We can follow and trace and move and act. We're always trying to be the noun in the sentence. Avoid being the direct object. Don't let things be done to you. And as we do all that doing, all that making and harvesting, all the procreating and fence-building, someone or something is being changed. As the doer, you pretend you can control the change.

But change is natural. Nature, both human and wild, responds to change with equilibrium. The change that happens to what you do to nature is what happens to the nature in you. The more we try to keep the wild outside, the more the wild seems to creep, in fiercer and in divided form, inside.

Third Tier

When the neighbor came over to the garage sale, he told me about his daughter. She is twenty-two and has breast cancer. I wonder if she is the female/minor in question. His wife, who I can see from the front porch, he told me, has blood clots. They're moving. I don't ask why. I imagined someone complained to the landlord and the landlord didn't want the stink of impure rent contaminating his wallet.

The day they moved out, it was just him carrying box after box. His wife, with the blood clots, couldn't lift anything. They packed their Rav 4 and their Pathfinder to the respective roofs. I didn't offer to help. But I did watch from my window and felt sorry for them. I hoped they would find a new place to live.

The wolves haven't entered Utah yet. I want to warn the wolves— stay in Idaho. Stay in Wyoming where the populations are lower so the mobilization against you will be quieter. I wish you could come here and make the forests where the Boy Scouts get lost, where the campers get hit by lightning, where climbers fall, and river runners drown, wild again. Wilder than they are. But the humans are everywhere and they are all armed. The cows and the sheep mill around, even on the road. The cows aren't armed with anything but size, but sometimes cars run into them and the drivers die. But then, sometimes, the cows die too.

I keep the fantasies, as natural and perverted though they may be. The one about the wolf roaming the Rockies and the one about the boy and the girl making out in the car pulled to the side of the road still tumble in my head like rocks in a polisher. It's natural to fantasize. Even unnatural and impossible fantasies. Sands shift. Things that were once white cliffs of sand turn to stone figurines. Sometimes fantasies come true. Sometimes, you stop pretending you could control either the fantasies or the sand. Sometimes you just mark—this happened. And then this. And so we call the lines in the sand limestone, soapstone, sandstone—each a colorful variant of the other.

Maybe you draw the line just asking, right or wrong? Fantasy or reality? Wolf or dog? Just bringing them together and looking at them in contrast might be enough to make the distinctions clear.

Or maybe it's in what you name things. Dog. Fantasy.

When Zoe was born, we named her Zoe, which means life. Whether natural or fantastical, that seemed like a good place to start.

ACKNOWLEDGMENTS

It's humbling to think how many people it takes to make a book. I'm not entirely sure why my name gets to go on the cover. I want to thank many people in my graduate program: Lynn Kilpatrick, Samantha Ruckman, David Hawkins, Jenn Gibbs, Susan Goslee, Traci O'Connor, Kathryn Cowles, Eric Burger, Kate Rosenberg, Maggie Golston, Heidi Czerwiec, Derek Pollard, Rebecca Lindenberg, Jenny Colville, Mary Anne Mohanraj, Paul Ketzle, Erin Sweeney, Trista Emmer, Mike White, Pam Balluck and especially the people in that first nonfiction class with Jeff Chapman, David McGlynn, Matthew Batt, Rachel Marston, Lauri Rouse, and Steve Tuttle—that was the beginning of this book and without them, I don't think it would have gotten off the ground. Julie Paegle, who keeps my writing head afloat. Steve Fellner who keeps me paddling forward. Margot Singer, who was also in that first nonfiction class and who is still my creative nonfiction writing co-conspirator. Ander Monson who read several versions of this book and deemed this one best. To Peter Covino who helped bring my first book into the world. To Brenda Miller who helped pave the way. To Rebecca Campbell who granted me the gift of her artwork for the cover and the early-on belief that she and I would do something big. Robin Hemley who always made me believe these essays would one day become a book of their own. David Shields who gave so much attention to this book out of simple generosity. Thanks to Misty Cummings who was the first to say, you're a real writer. Thanks to Katharine Coles and Karen Brennan for mentoring me through genres and back again. To Ann Cummins, Jane Armstrong, Allen Woodman and Barbara Anderson who brought me to NAU to teach what I write. To Beya Thayer who reads what I write and reminds me to write outdoors. To Rick and Eleanor who gave me the time to write, and extra thanks to El who read every word. Susan Wallace and Amy Wright for bringing the book into daylight. To Lia Purpura who chose this book to win Zone 3's first creative nonfiction prize and whose work inspires me. My sisters Paige Walker and Valerie Elgart who embrace my many book projects and were the first champions of this one. I'm grateful for my mom, Janice Walker, for believing writing is a worthy vocation and for reading this with such generosity. For Erik Sather for believing in everything I do. For Max and Zoe who share their time with this writing business and inspire me to write better every day. I'm truly honored by all who have helped me to make this book. It deserves coming into being thanks to you.